KU-044-326

ELT documents
111 - Issues in Language Testing

Editors: J Charles Alderson
Arthur Hughes

The British Council
Central Information Service
English Language and Literature Division

The opinions expressed in this volume are those of the authors and do not necessarily reflect the opinion of the British Council.

ELT Documents is now including a correspondence section. Comments arising from articles in current issues will therefore be most welcome. Please address comments to ELSD, The British Council, 10 Spring Gardens, London SW1A 2BN.

The articles and information in *ELT Documents* are copyright but permission will generally be granted for use in whole or in part by educational establishments. Enquiries should be directed to the British Council, Design, Production and Publishing Department, 65 Davies Street, London W1Y 2AA.

ISBN 0 901618 51 9

© The British Council 1981

CONTENTS

SECTION 3: General Language Proficiency

INTRODUCTION

This book arose from an occasion in October 1980 when seven applied linguists met in Lancaster to discuss what they felt were important problems in the assessment of learning a second or foreign language. This Symposium resulted, partly because of its informal nature and its deliberately small size, in an intense discussion in certain areas, a concentration which is rarely possible in conferences or large seminars. It was felt that the Symposium had been so useful that it was decided to make the discussion public, in order not only to let others know what had happened at Lancaster, but also to encourage and stimulate a much broader and hopefully even richer debate in the areas touched upon.

Testing has become an area of increased interest to language teachers and applied linguists in the last decade. Yet as Davies says (Davies 1979) testing has for many years firmly resisted attempts to bring it within the mainstream of applied linguistics. This is no doubt to some extent due to historical reasons, as both Davies and Morrow (this volume) suggest. In the era that Spolsky dubbed the 'psychometric-structuralist period' language testing was dominated by criteria for the establishment of educational measuring instruments developed within the tradition of psychometrics. As a result of this emphasis on the statistical analysis of language tests, a group developed, over the years, of specialists in language testing, 'Testing Experts', popularly believed to live in an arcane world of numbers and formulae. As most language teachers are from a non-numerate background (sometimes having deliberately fled 'figures') it is not surprising that they were reluctant to involve themselves in the mysteries of statistics. Consequently, an expertise developed in language testing and particularly proficiency testing, divorced from the concerns of the language classroom, and imbued with its own separate concerns and values which to outsiders were only partially comprehensible and apparently irrelevant. Despite the advent of Spolsky's third phase of language testing — the psycholinguistic-sociolinguistic phase (what Moller (this volume) calls the third and fourth phases — psycholinguistic-sociolinguistic and sociolinguistic-communicative phases) — 'testing' has not yet recovered from this image of being stubbornly irrelevant to or unconcerned with the language teacher, except for its embodiment in 'exams' which dominate many a syllabus (be it the Cambridge First Certificate or the TOEFL). Teachers who **have** felt they should be concerned with assessing what or whether learners have learned have found the jargon and argument—ation of 'Testing' forbidding and obscure.

But evaluation (note how the terminology has changed over the years, with the intention of making the subject less threatening) is readily acknowledged by teachers and curriculum theorists alike to be an essential part of language learning, just as feedback is recognised as essential in any learning process. The consequence of this need to evaluate has been the fact that teachers have actually carried out tests all along but have felt uncomfortable, indeed guilty and apologetic about doing so when there is apparently so much about 'testing' they do not know. So when suggesting that 'Testing' has become more central to the present-day concerns of language teachers, it is not intended to imply that previously — 'in the bad old days' — nobody tested, or that the testing that was done was of ill repute, but merely to suggest that teachers felt that what they were doing was in some important sense lacking in respectability however relevant or important it might actually have been. The fact is, however, that testing has become an area of increased research activity, and many more articles are published on the subject today in professional journals than ten years ago. This is evidence of a turning in the tide of applied linguistics towards more empirical concerns.

It has been suggested that testing has to date remained outside the mainstream of applied linguistics; in particular, the view of language incorporated in many tests has become increasingly at odds with theories of language and language use — indeed, to some extent at least, it no longer reflects classroom practice in language teaching. Now there may be good arguments for tests not to follow the whim of fashion in language teaching, but when there is a serious discrepancy between the teaching and the means of evaluating that teaching, then something appears to be amiss. The feeling abroad today is that theories abound of communicative language teaching, of the teaching of ESP, of integrated language teaching, but where are the tests to operationalise those theories? Where are the communicative language tests, the ESP tests, the integrated language tests? Applied linguists and language teachers alike are making increasingly insistent demands on language testers to supply the language tests that current theory and practice require, and the response of testers has, to date, been mixed. Some have rushed in where others have feared to tread: extravagant claims have been made for new techniques, new tests, new assessment procedures. Others have stubbornly resisted the pressure, claiming that tests of communicative competence or ESP are either impossible (in theory, or in practice) or unnecessary because existing tests and techniques are entirely adequate. Inevitably, there are also agnostics on the side lines, who remain sceptical until they have seen the evidence for and against the claims of either side.

This book is for those agnostics, though believers and non-believers alike may find something of interest. The Symposium at Lancaster was an attempt to focus, without taking sides, on areas of major concern to teachers and testers at present:

communicative language testing,
the testing of English for Specific Purposes,
the testing of general language proficiency.

It was hoped by intense debate to establish what the important issues were in these areas, so that the interested reader could provide himself with a set of criteria for judging (or constructing) language tests, or perhaps more realistically, for investigating further. It is clear, always, that more research is needed but it is hoped that this book will help to clarify where research and development needs to be concentrated at present. We are living in a world of claim and counter-claim, where the excitement of the battle may make us lose sight of the reasons for the conflict: namely the need for learners and outsiders to assess progress in language learning or **potential** for such progress, as accurately as possible. No research programme or test development should forget this.

The format of the Symposium was as follows. Having decided on the three main areas for debate, recent and influential articles in those areas were selected for study and all Symposium participants were asked to produce papers reacting to one or more of these articles, outlining what they felt to be the important issues being raised. These reaction papers were circulated in advance of the Symposium, and the Symposium itself consisted of a discussion in each of the three areas, based on the original articles and the related reaction papers.

Like the Symposium, the volume is divided into three main sections: one section for each of the areas of communicative language testing, ESP testing, and general language proficiency. Within each section there are three parts: the original article(s), the reaction papers and an account of the discussion based upon tape recordings of the proceedings by the present writer. These accounts of the discussion do not represent the views of any one participant, including the present writer, but are an attempt to summarise the issues that were raised. However, it should be stressed that although the accounts of the discussion attempt to be fair to the substance and quality of the debate, they must, inevitably, ultimately represent one person's view of what was said, since it would be impossible to achieve complete consensus on what was said, let alone its correctness or significance. At times the accounts repeat points made in the reaction papers also published in this volume, but no apologies are offered for repetition, as this simply reflects the level of interest in or concern over these particular points. Although it was hoped to include responses from the authors of the original articles only one response was available at the time of going to press, that of Helmut Vollmer. Nevertheless, it is hoped that subsequent debate will include the responses and further thoughts of the other authors in the light of these discussions.

This is not a definitive volume on language testing — and it does not attempt to be such. What this book hopes to do is to encourage further debate, a critical or sceptical approach to claims made about 'progress' and 'theories', and to encourage practical research in important areas.

It has not been the intention of this Introduction to guide the reader through the discussions — that would have been presumptuous and unnecessary — but rather to set the scene for them. Thus there is here no summary of positions taken, arguments developed and issues raised. However, there is, after the three main sections, an Epilogue, and the reader is advised not to ignore this: it is intended, not to tell the reader what he has read, but to point the way forward in the ongoing debate about the assessment of language learning. 'Testing' should not and cannot be left to 'Testers': one of the most encouraging developments of the last decade is the involvement of more applied linguists in the area of assessment and evaluation. In a sense, there can be no Epilogue, because the debate is unfinished, and we hope that participation in the debate will grow. It is ultimately up to the reader to write his own 'Way Forward'.

Thanks are due to all Symposium participants, not only for their contributions, written and spoken, to the Symposium, but also for their help in preparing this volume. Thanks are also due to the Institute for English Language Education, Lancaster, for hosting the Symposium and contributing materially to the preparation of this book.

J Charles Alderson,
University of Lancaster

SECTION 1

COMMUNICATIVE LANGUAGE TESTING: REVOLUTION OR EVOLUTION?[1]
Keith Morrow, Bell School of Languages, Norwich

Introduction

Wilkins (1976) concludes with the observation that, 'we do not know how to establish the communicative proficiency of the learner' and expresses the hope that, 'while some people are experimenting with the notional syllabus as such, others should be attempting to develop the new testing techniques that should, ideally, accompany it' (*loc cit*). In the two years that have passed since the publication of this book, the author's hope on the one hand has been increasingly realised, and if his observation on the other is still valid, there are grounds for believing that it will not be so for much longer.

At the time of writing, it is probably true to say that there exists a considerable imbalance between the resources available to language teachers (at least in E F L) in terms of teaching materials, and those available in terms of testing and evaluation instruments. The former have not been slow to incorporate insights into syllabus design, and increasingly methodology, deriving from a view of language as communication; the latter still reflect, on the whole, ideas about language and how it should be tested which fail to take account of these recent developments in any systematic way.[2]

This situation does seem to be changing, however. A number of institutions and organisations have set up working parties to assess the feasibility of tests based on communicative criteria, and in some cases these have moved on to

---

[1] This article was first published in *The Communicative approach to language teaching* ed: C J Brumfit and K Johnson. Oxford University Press, 1979. Reprinted here by kind permission of Oxford University Press.

[2] Exceptions to this are the two oral examinations promoted by the Association of Recognised English Language Schools: The ARELS Certificate and the ARELS Diploma, as well as the Joint Matriculation Board's Test in English for Overseas Students. But without disrespect to these, I would claim that they do not meet in a rigorous way some of the criteria established later in this paper.

the design stage.[3] It therefore seems reasonable to expect that over the next five years new tests and examinations will become available which will aim to do precisely the job which Wilkins so recently held up as a challenge, ie to measure communicative proficiency.

This paper, then, will be concerned with the implications for test design and construction of the desire to measure communicative proficiency, and with the extent to which earlier testing procedures need to be reviewed and reconsidered in the light of this objective. But it is a polemical paper. The assumption which underlies it is that the measurement of communicative proficiency is a job worth doing, and the task is ultimately a feasible one.

The Vale of Tears

A wide range of language tests and examinations are currently in use but most belong to a few key types. Spolsky (1975) identifies three stages in the recent history of language testing: the pre-scientific, the psychometric-structuralist, and the psycholinguistic-sociolinguistic. We might characterise these in turn as the Garden of Eden, the Vale of Tears and the Promised Land, and different tests (indeed different parts of the same test) can usually be seen to relate to one or other of these stages. The historical perspective offered by Spolsky is extremely relevant to the concerns of this paper. While critiques of the 'prescientific' approach to testing are already familiar (Valette, 1967), it seems useful to take some time here to clarify the extent to which current developments relate to what has more immediately gone before through a critical look at some of the characteristics of psychometric-structuralist testing. The point of departure for this is Lado (1961).

Atomistic

A key feature of Lado's approach is the breaking down of the complexities of language into isolated segments. This influences both what is to be tested and how this testing should be carried out.

What is to be tested is revealed by a structural contrastive analysis between the target language and the learner's mother tongue. Structural here is not limited to grammatical structure — though this is of course important.

---

[3] My own work in this field has been sponsored by the Royal Society of Arts who have established a Working Party to re-design their range of examinations for foreign students. The English Language Testing Service of the British Council is developing communicative tests in the area of English for Academic Purposes, and a similar line is likely to be followed soon by the Associated Examining Board.

Contrastive analysis can be carried out of all the levels of structure (syntactic down to phonological) which the language theory encompasses, and test items can be constructed on the basis of them.

The same approach is adopted to the question of how to test. Discrete items are constructed, each of which ideally reveals the candidate's ability to handle one level of the language in terms of one of the four skills. It soon became recognised that it was in fact extremely difficult to construct 'pure' test items which were other than exceedingly trivial in nature, and thus many tests of this sort contain items which operate on more than one level of structure.

The clear advantage of this form of test construction is that it yields data which are easily quantifiable. But the problem is equally clearly that its measurement of language proficiency depends crucially upon the assumption that such proficiency is neatly quantifiable in this way. Indeed the general problem with Lado's approach, which attaches itself very firmly to certain very definite views about the nature of language, is that it crumbles like a house of cards as soon as the linguistic foundation on which it is constructed is attacked. This is not the place to develop a generalised linguistic attack, but one particular assumption is worth picking up, since it is so central to the issue under discussion.

An atomistic approach to test design depends utterly on the assumption that knowledge of the elements of a language is equivalent to knowledge of the language. Even if one adopts for the moment a purely grammatical view of what it is to know a language (cf Chomsky's definition in terms of the ability to formulate all and only the grammatical sentences in a language), then it seems fairly clear that a vital stage is missing from an atomistic analysis, viz the ability to synthesise. Knowledge of the elements of a language in fact counts for nothing unless the user is able to combine them in new and appropriate ways to meet the linguistic demands of the situation in which he wishes to use the language. Driving a car is a skill of a quite different order from that of performing in isolation the various movements of throttle, brake, clutch, gears and steering wheel.

Quantity v. Quality

In the previous section it was the linguistic basis of tests such as Lado's which was questioned. Let us now turn to the psychological implications. Following the behaviourist view of learning through habit formation, Lado's tests pose questions to elicit responses which show whether or not correct habits have been established. Correct responses are rewarded and negative ones punished in some way. Passing a test involves making a specified proportion of correct responses. Clearly language learning is viewed as a process of accretion.

An alternative view of the psychology of language learning would hold, however, that the answers to tests can, and should, be considered as more than simply right or wrong. In this view learners possess 'transitional competence' (Corder, 1975) which enables them to produce and use an 'interlanguage' (Selinker, 1972). Like the competence of a native speaker, this is an essentially dynamic concept and the role of the test is to show how far it has moved towards an approximation of a native speaker's system. Tests will thus be concerned with making the learner produce samples of his own 'interlanguage', based on his own norms of language production so that conclusions can be drawn from it. Tests of receptive skills will similarly be concerned with revealing the extent to which the candidate's processing abilities match those of a native speaker.

The clear implication of this is that the candidate's responses need to be assessed not quantitatively, but qualitatively. Tests should be designed to reveal not simply the number of items which are answered correctly, but to reveal the quality of the candidate's language performance. It is not safe to assume that a given score on the former necessarily allows conclusions to be drawn about the latter.

Reliability

One of the most significant features of psychometric tests as opposed to those of 'pre-scientific' days is the development of the twin concepts of reliability and validity.

The basis of the reliability claimed by Lado is objectivity. The rather obvious point has, however, not escaped observers (Pilliner, 1968; Robinson, 1973) that Lado's tests are objective only in terms of actual assessment. In terms of the evaluation of the numerical score yielded, and perhaps more importantly, in terms of the construction of the test itself, subjective factors play a large part.

It has been equally noted by observers that an insistence on testing procedures which can be objectively assessed has a number of implications for the data yielded. Robinson (*op cit*) identifies three areas of difference between testing procedures designed to yield data which can be objectively assessed and those which are open to subjective assessment.

1   The amount of language produced by the student. In an objective test, students may actually produce no language at all. Their role may be limited to selecting alternatives rather than producing language.

2   Thus the type of ability which is being tested is crucially different. In a subjective test the candidate's ability to produce language is a crucial factor; in an objective test the ability to recognise appropriate forms is sufficient.

3   The norms of language use are established on different grounds. In an objective test the candidate must base his responses upon the language of the examiner; in a subjective test, the norms may be his own, deriving from his own use of the language. Thus an objective test can reveal only differences and similarities between the language norms of the examiner and candidate; it can tell us nothing of the norms which the candidate himself would apply in a use situation.

The above factors lead to what Davies (1978) has called the reliability-validity 'tension'. Attempts to increase the reliability of tests have led test designers to take an over-restrictive view of what it is that they are testing.

Validity

The idea that language test designers should concern themselves with validity — in other words that they should ask themselves whether they are actually testing what they think they are testing, and whether what they think they are testing is what they ought to be testing — is clearly an attractive one. But unfortunately, because of the 'tension' referred to above, designers working within the tradition we are discussing seem to have been content with answers to these questions which are less than totally convincing.

Five types of validity which a language test may claim are traditionally identified (cf Davies, 1968).

Face	the test looks like a good one.
Content	the test accurately reflects the syllabus on which it is based.
Predictive	the test accurately predicts performance in some subsequent situation.
Concurrent	the test gives similar results to existing tests which have already been validated.
Construct	the test reflects accurately the principles of a valid theory of foreign language learning.

Statistical techniques for assessing validity in these terms have been developed to a high, and often esoteric level of sophistication. But unfortunately, with two exceptions (face, and possibly predictive) the types of validity outlined above are all ultimately circular. Starting from a certain set of assumptions about the nature of language and language learning will lead to language tests which are perfectly valid in terms of these assumptions, but whose value must inevitably be called into question if the basic assumptions themselves are challenged. Thus a test which perfectly satisfies criteria of content, construct or concurrent validity may nonetheless fail to show in any interesting way how well a candidate can perform in or use the target language. This may occur quite simply if the construct of the language learning theory, and the content of the syllabus are themselves not related to this aim, or if the test is validated against other language tests which do not concern themselves with this objective. There is clearly no such thing in testing as 'absolute' validity. Validity exists only in terms of specified criteria, and if the criteria turn out to be the wrong ones, then validity claimed in terms of them turns out to be spurious. *Caveat emptor.*

Comments

This criticism, implicit and explicit, made in the preceding sections applies to a theory of testing which has hardly ever been realised in the extreme form in which Lado presented it. Certainly in the U.K., a mixture of pragmatism and conservatism has ensured that much of the institutionalised testing of foreign languages owes as much to the 1920's as to the 1960's. This does not mean though, that there is anything chimerical about the ideas put forward by Lado. Their influence has been recognised by writers on language testing ever since the first publication of his book. But it is as representation of theory that the ideas are most significant. In practice, as Davies (1978) remarks, there is very often a gap between what Lado himself does and what he says he does.

But this gap is often of detail rather than principle. Even if the totality of Lado's views have been more often honoured in the breach than in the observance, the influence of his work has been tremendous. Of the ideas examined above, very few have failed to find implicit acceptance in the majority of 'theory-based' tests developed over the last fifteen years. The overriding importance of reliability (hence the ubiquitous multiple-choice), the acceptance of validity of a statistical rather than necessarily of a practical nature, the directly quantifiable modes of assessment — these are all ideas which have become common currency even among those who would reject many of the theories of language and language learning on which Lado based his approach.

Only in one area has a consistent alternative to Lado's views been argued, and that is the development of 'integrated' tests/test items[4] as opposed to Lado's arguments (at least in principle) in favour of 'pure' discrete items.[5] A clear statement of an 'integrated' position is made by Carroll (1968):

> '. . . since the use of language in ordinary situations call upon all these aspects [of language], we must further recognise that linguistic performance also involves the individual's capability of mobilizing his linguistic competences and performance abilities in an integrated way, ie in the understanding, speaking, reading or writing of connected discourse.'

This implies a view of language which runs directly counter to a key assumption which we have earlier examined in Lado's work. It denies the atomistic nature of language as a basis for language testing. To this extent, Carroll's contribution is extremely important, but even here it must be observed that in practical terms he was doing no more than providing a post-hoc rationalisation. For the purely practical reasons alluded to earlier, very few 'pure' items had found their way into tests; in a sense, Carroll was merely legitimising the existing situation.

Less casuistically, it must be observed that attempts to develop more revolutionary integrated tests (Oller, 1971, 1973) have left out of account a crucial element in the original formulation, viz. 'the use of language in ordinary situations'.

Both cloze and dictation are fundamentally tests of language competence. Both have their uses in determining the basic level of language proficiency of a given candidate. (More accurately, they enable the level of language proficiency to be assessed relative to that of other people who take exactly the same test under the same conditions.) Oller claims that both test basic language processing mechanisms (analysis by synthesis); both sample a wide range of structural and lexical items in a meaningful context. But neither

---

[4] Note that the word 'integrated' is used in different ways by different writers. For some it is possible to conceive of individual items which test integration of various elements of the language; for others the very isolation of separate items means that full integration is not being achieved.

[5] Earlier it was implied that Lado himself very rarely used items of a totally pure kind. See Davies (1978) for an interesting discussion of integrated v. discrete-point testing. Davies argues that they are at different ends of the same continuum rather than in different universes.

gives any convincing proof of the candidate's ability to actually use the language, to translate the competence (or lack of it) which he is demonstrating into actual performance 'in ordinary situations', ie actually using the language to read, write, speak or listen in ways and contexts which correspond to real life.

Adopting this 'use' criterion might lead us to consider precisely why neither discrete-point nor integrative tests of the type we have considered are able to meet it.

Let us look in a rather simple way at some of the features of language use which do not seem to be measured in conventional tests.

Interaction — Based: in the vast majority of cases, language in use is based on an interaction. Even cases such as letter writing, which may seem to be solitary activities, can be considered as weak forms of interaction in that they involve an addressee, whose expectations will be taken into account by the writer. These expectations will affect both the content of the message and the way in which it is expressed. A more characteristic form of interaction, however, is represented by face-to-face oral interaction which involves not only the modification of expression and content mentioned above but also an amalgam of receptive and productive skills. What is said **by** a speaker depends crucially on what is said **to** him.

Unpredictability: the apparently trivial observation that the development of an interaction is unpredictable is in fact extremely significant for the language user. The processing of unpredictable data in real time is a vital aspect of using language.

Context: any use of language will take place in a context, and the language forms which are appropriate will vary in accordance with this context. Thus a language user must be able to handle appropriacy in terms of:

context of situation	eg	physical environment
		role/status of participants
		attitude/formality
linguistic context	eg	textual cohesion

Purpose: a rather obvious feature of communication is that every utterance is made for a purpose. Thus a language user must be able to recognise why a certain remark has been addressed to him, and be able to encode appropriate utterances to achieve his own purposes.

Performance: What Chomsky (1965) described as 'competence', leaving out of account:

'such grammatically irrelevant conditions as memory limitations, distractions, shifts of attention and interest, and errors (random or characteristic)'

has been the basis of most language tests. Such conditions may or may not be 'grammatically irrelevant', but they certainly exist. To this extent the idealised language presented in listening tests fails to measure the effectiveness of the candidate's strategies for receptive performance. Similarly, the demand for context-free language production fails to measure the extent to which features of the candidate's performance may in fact hamper communication.

Authenticity: a very obvious feature of authentic language should be noted in this context, ie with rare exceptions it is not simplified to take account of the linguistic level of the addressee. Thus measuring the ability of the candidate to, eg read a simplified text tells us nothing about his actual communicative ability, since an important feature of such ability is precisely the capacity to come to terms with what is unknown.

Behaviour-Based: the success or failure of an interaction is judged by its participants on the basis of behavioural outcomes. Strictly speaking no other criteria are relevant. This is an extreme view of the primacy of content over form in language and would probably be criticised by language teachers. Nevertheless, more emphasis needs to be placed in a communicative context on the notion of behaviour. A test of communication must take as its starting point the measurement of what the candidate can actually achieve through language. None of the tests we have considered have set themselves this task.

These then are some of the characteristics of language in use as communication which existing tests fail to measure or to take account of in a systematic way. Let us now turn to an examination of some of the implications of building them into the design specification for language tests.

The Promised Land

We can expect a test of communicative ability to have at least the following characteristics:

1 It will be criterion-referenced against the operational performance of a set of authentic language tasks. In other words it will set out to show whether or not (or how well) the candidate can perform a set of specified activities.

2   It will be crucially concerned to establish its own validity as a measure of those operations it claims to measure. Thus content, construct and predictive validity will be important, but concurrent validity with existing tests will not be necessarily significant.

3   It will rely on modes of assessment which are not directly quantitative, but which are instead qualitative. It may be possible or necessary to convert these into numerical scores, but the process is an indirect one and recognised as such.

4   Reliability, while clearly important, will be subordinate to face validity. Spurious objectivity will no longer be a prime consideration, although it is recognised that in certain situations test formats which can be assessed mechanically will be advantageous. The limitations of such formats will be clearly spelt out, however.

Designing a test with these characteristics raises a number of interesting issues.

Performance Tests

Asking the question, 'What can this candidate do?' clearly implies a performance-based test. The idea that performance (rather than competence) is a legitimate area of concern for tests is actually quite a novel one and poses a number of problems, chiefly in terms of extrapolation and assessment. If one assesses a candidate's performance in terms of a particular task, what does one learn of his ability to perform other tasks? Unless ways of doing this in some effective way can be found, operational tests which are economical in terms of time are likely to run the risk of being trivial. Problems of assessment are equally fundamental. Performance is by its very nature an integrated phenomenon and any attempt to isolate and test discrete elements of it destroys the essential holism. Therefore a quantitative assessment procedure is necessarily impractical and some form of qualitative assessment must be found. This has obvious implications for reliability.

Given these problems, the question obviously arises as to whether communicative testing does necessarily involve performance tests. This seems to depend on what the purpose of the test is. If the purpose is proficiency testing, ie if one is asking how successful the candidate is likely to be as a user of the language in some general sense, then it seems to be incontrovertible that performance tests are necessary. The reasons for saying this should by now be clear, but at the risk of labouring the point let me re-state the principle that in language use the whole is bigger than the parts. No matter how sophisticated the analysis of the parts, no matter whether the parts are isolated in terms of structures, lexis or functions, it is implausible to derive hard data about actual language performance from tests of control of these parts alone. However, if the test is to be used for diagnostic purposes rather than proficiency assessment, a rather different set of considerations may apply. In a diagnostic situation it may become important not simply to know the degree of skill which a candidate can bring to the performance of a particular global task, but also to find out precisely which of the communicative skills and elements of the language he has mastered. To the extent that these can be revealed by discrete-point tests and that the deficiencies so revealed might form the input to a teaching programme, this might be information worth having. (The form that such tests might take is discussed in Morrow, 1977.) But one more point must be made. It might be argued that discrete-point tests of the type under discussion are useful as achievement tests, ie to indicate the degree of success in assimilating the content of a language learning programme which is itself based on a communicative (notional) syllabus. This seems to me misguided. As a pedagogic device a notional syllabus may specify the elements which are to be mastered for communicative purposes. But there is little value in assimilating these elements if they cannot be integrated into meaningful language performance. Therefore discrete-point tests are of little worth in this context.

The clear implication of the preceding paragraphs is that by and large it is performance tests which are of most value in a communicative context. The very real problems of extrapolation and assessment raised at the beginning of this section therefore have to be faced. To what extent do they oblige us to compromise our principle?

Let us deal first with extrapolation. A model for the performance of global communicative tasks may show for any task the enabling skills which have to be mobilised to complete it. Such a model is implicit in Munby (1978) and has been refined for testing purposes by B J Carroll (1978). An example of the way this might work is as follows:

Global Task

    Search text for specific information

Enabling Skills

eg Distinguish main point from supporting details
   Understand text relations through grammatical cohesion devices
   Understand relations within sentences
   Understand conceptual meaning
   Deduce meaning of unfamiliar lexis

The status of these enabling skills *vis-à-vis* competence:performance is interesting. They may be identified by an analysis of performance in operational terms, and thus they are clearly, ultimately performance-based. But at the same time, their application extends far beyond any one particular instance of performance and in this creativity they reflect an aspect of what is generally understood by competence. In this way they offer a possible approach to the problem of extrapolation.

An analysis of the global tasks in terms of which the candidate is to be assessed (see later) will usually yield a fairly consistent set of enabling skills. Assessment of ability in using these skills therefore yields data which are relevant across a broad spectrum of global tasks, and are not limited to a single instance of performance.

While assessment based on these skills strictly speaking offends against the performance criterion which we have established, it should be noted that the skills are themselves operational in that they derive from an analysis of task performance. It is important that the difference between discrete-point tests of these enabling skills and discrete-point tests of structural aspects of the language system is appreciated.

Clearly, though, there exists in tests of enabling skills a fundamental weakness which is reminiscent of the problem raised in connection with earlier structural tests, namely the relationship between the whole and the parts. It is conceivable that a candidate may prove quite capable of handling individual enabling skills, and yet prove quite incapable of mobilising them in a use situation or developing appropriate strategies to communicate effectively. Thus we seem to be forced back on tests of performance.

A working solution to this problem seems to be the development of tests which measure both overall performance in relation to a specified task, and the strategies and skills which have been used in achieving it. Written and spoken production can be assessed in terms of both these criteria. In task-based tests of listening and reading comprehension, however, it may be rather more difficult to see just how the global task has been completed. For example, in a test based on the global task exemplified above and which has the format of a number of true/false questions which the candidate has to answer by searching through a text, it is rather difficult to assess why a particular answer has been given and to deduce the skills and strategies employed. In such cases questions focusing on specific enabling skills do seem to be called for in order to provide the basis for convincing extrapolation.

If this question of the relationship between performance and the way it is achieved, and the testing strategy which it is legitimate to adopt in order to measure it seems to have been dealt with at inordinate length in the context of this paper, this reflects my feeling that here is the central distinction between what has gone before and what is now being proposed.

Admitting the necessity for tests of performance immediately raises the problem of assessment. How does one judge production in ways which are not hopelessly subjective, and how does one set receptive tasks appropriate for different levels of language proficiency?

The answer seems to lie in the concept of an operational scale of attainment, in which different levels of proficiency are defined in terms of a set of performance criteria. The most interesting work I know of in this area has been carried out by B J Carroll (Carroll, 1977). In this, Carroll distinguishes different levels of performance by matching the candidate's performance with operational specifications which take account of the following parameters:

Size Complexity	} of text which can be handled
Range	of, eg enabling skills, structures, functions which can be handled
Speed	at which language can be processed
Flexibility	Shown in dealing with changes of, eg topic
Accuracy Appropriacy	} with which, eg enabling skills, structures, functions, can be handled
Independence	from reference sources and interlocutor
Repetition Hesitation	} in processing text

These specifications (despite the difficulties of phrasing them to take account of this in the summary given) are related to both receptive and productive performance.

It may well be that these specifications need to be refined in practice, but they seem to offer a way of assessing the quality of performance at different levels in a way which combines face validity with at least potential reliability. This question of reliability is of course central. As yet there are no published data on the degree of marker reliability which can be achieved using a scheme of this sort, but informal experience suggests that standardisation meetings should enable fairly consistent scorings to be achieved. One important factor is obviously the form which these scores should take and the precise basis on which they should be arrived at.

It would be possible to use an analytic system whereby candidates' performance was marked in terms of each of the criteria in turn and these were then totalled to give a score. More attractive (to me at least) is a scheme whereby an overall impression mark is given with the marker instructed simply to base his impression on the specified criteria. Which of these will work better in practice remains to be seen, but the general point may be made that the first belongs to a quantitative, analytic tradition, the second to a qualitative, synthetic approach.

Content

We have so far considered some of the implications of a performance-based approach to testing, but have avoided the central issue: what performance? The general point to make in this connection is perhaps that there is no general answer.

One of the characteristic features of the communicative approach to language teaching is that it obliges us (or enables us) to make assumptions about the types of communication we will equip learners to handle. This applies equally to communicative testing.

This means that there is unlikely to be, in communicative terms, a single overall test of language proficiency. What will be offered are tests of proficiency (at different levels) in terms of specified communicative criteria. There are three important implications in this. First, the concept of pass:fail loses much of its force; every candidate can be assessed in terms of what he can do. Of course some will be able to do more than others, and it may be decided for administrative reasons that a certain level of proficiency is necessary for the awarding of a particular certificate. But because of the operational nature of the test, even low scorers can be shown what they have achieved. Secondly, language performance can be differentially assessed in different communicative areas. The idea of 'profile reporting' whereby a candidate is given different scores on, eg speaking, reading, writing and listening tests is not new, but it is particularly attractive in an operational context where scores can be related to specific communicative objectives.

The third implication is perhaps the most far-reaching. The importance of specifying the communicative criteria in terms of which assessment is being offered means that examining bodies will have to draw up, and probably publish, specifications of the types of operation they intend to test, the content areas to which they will relate and the criteria which will be adopted in assessment. Only if this is done will the test be able to claim to know what it is measuring, and only in this way will the test be able to show meaningfully what a candidate can do.

The design of a communicative test can thus be seen as involving the answers to the following questions:

1   What are the performance operations we wish to test? These are arrived at by considering what sorts of things people actually use language for in the areas in which we are interested.

2   At what level of proficiency will we expect the candidate to perform these operations?

3   What are the enabling skills involved in performing these operations? Do we wish to test control of these separately?

4   What sort of content areas are we going to specify? This will affect both the types of operation and the types of 'text'[6] which are appropriate.

5   What sort of format will we adopt for the questions we set? It must be one which allows for both reliability and face validity as a test of language use.

Conclusion

The only conclusion which is necessary is to say that no conclusion is necessary. The rhetorical question posed by the title is merely rhetoric. After all it matters little if the developments I have tried to outline are actually evolutionary. But my own feeling is that those (eg Davies, 1978) who minimise the differences between different approaches to testing are adopting a viewpoint which is perhaps too comfortable; I think there is some blood to be spilt yet.

---

[6]Use of the term 'text' may mislead the casual reader into imagining that only the written language is under discussion. In fact the question of text type is relevant to both the written and the spoken language in both receptive and productive terms. In the written mode it is clear that types of text may be specified in terms such as 'genre' and 'topic' as belonging to a certain set in relation to which performance may be assessed; specifying spoken texts may be less easy, since the categories that should be applied in an analysis of types of talking are less well established. I am at present working in a framework which applies certain macro-functions (eg ideational, directive, interpersonal) to a model of interaction which differentiates between speaker-centred and listener-centred speech. It is hoped that this will allow us to specify clearly enough the different types of talking candidates will be expected to deal with. More problematical is the establishing of different role-relationships in an examination context and the possibility of testing the candidates' production of anything but rather formal stranger:stranger language. Simulation techniques, while widely used for pedagogic purposes, may offend against the authenticity of performance criterion we have established, though it is possible that those who are familiar with them may be able to compensate for this.

BIBLIOGRAPHY

CARROLL, J B
The psychology of language testing. In: DAVIES A, ed (1968), *qv.*

CHOMSKY, N
Aspects of the theory of syntax. MIT Press, 1965.

CORDER, S P
Error analysis, interlanguage and second language acquisition. Language teaching and linguistics abstracts, Vol. 8, no. 4, 1975.

DAVIES, A, ed
Language testing symposium. London: Oxford University Press, 1968.

DAVIES, A
Language testing. Language teaching and linguistics abstracts, Vol. 11, nos. 3/4, 1978.

MORROW, K
Techniques of evaluation for a notional syllabus. Royal Society of Arts (mimeo), 1977.

OLLER, J
Dictation as a device for testing foreign language proficiency. English language teaching journal, Vol. 25, no. 3, 1971.

OLLER, J
Cloze tests of second language proficiency and what they measure. Language learning, Vol. 23, no. 1, 1973.

PILLINER, A E G
Subjective and objective testing. In: DAVIES, A, ed (1968), *qv.*

ROBINSON, P
Oral expression tests. English language teaching, Vol. 25, nos. 2 - 3, 1973.

SELINKER, L
Interlanguage. International review of applied linguistics, Vol. 10, no. 3, 1972.

SPOLSKY, B
Language testing: art or science? Paper presented at the Fourth AILA International Congress, Stuttgart, 1975.

VALETTE, R M
Modern language testing: a handbook. Harcourt Brace & World, 1967.

WILKINS, D A
Notional syllabuses. Oxford University Press, 1976.

REACTION TO THE MORROW PAPER (1)

Cyril J Weir, Associated Examining Board

Three questions need to be answered by those professing adherence to this 'new wave' in language testing:

1 What is communicative testing?
2 Is it a job worth doing?
3 Is it feasible?

1 What is communicative testing?

There is a compelling need to achieve a wider consensus on the use of terminology in both the testing and teaching of language if epithets such as 'communicative' are to avoid becoming as debased as other terms such as 'structure' have in EFL metalanguage. Effort must be made to establish more explicitly what it is we are referring to, especially in our use of key terms such as 'competence' and 'performance', if we are to be more confident in the claims we make concerning what it is that we are testing.

Canale and Swain (1980) provide us with a useful starting point for a clarification of the terminology necessary for forming a more definite picture of the construct, communicative testing. They take communicative competence to include grammatical competence (knowledge of the rules of grammar), sociolinguistic competence (knowledge of the rules of use and rules of discourse) and strategic competence (knowledge of verbal and non-verbal communication strategies). In Morrow's paper a further distinction is stressed between communicative competence and communicative performance, the distinguishing feature of the latter being the fact that performance is the realisation of Canale and Swain's (1980) three competences and their interaction:

'. . . in the actual production and comprehension of utterances under the general psychological constraints that are unique to performances.'

Morrow agrees with Canale and Swain (1980) that communicative language testing must be devoted not only to what the learner knows about the form of the language and about how to use it appropriately in contexts of use (**competence**), but must also consider the extent to which the learner is actually able to demonstrate this knowledge in a meaningful communicative

26

situation (**performance**) ie what he can do with the language, or as Rea (1978) puts it, his

> '. . . ability to communicate with ease and effect in specified sociolinguistic settings.'

It is held that the performance tasks candidates might be faced with in communicative tests should be representative of the type they might encounter in their own real world situation and would correspond to normal language use where an integration of communicative skills is required with little time to reflect on or monitor language input and output.

If we accept Morrow's distinction between tests of competence and performance and agree with him that the latter is now a legitimate area for concern in language testing, then this has quite far-reaching ramifications for future testing operations. For if we support the construct of performance based tests then in future far greater emphasis will be placed on the ability to communicate, and as Rea (1978) points out, language requirements will need to be expressed in functional terms and it will be necessary to provide operationally defined information on a candidate's test proficiency. Morrow raises the interesting possibility that in view of the importance of specifying the communicative criteria in terms of which assessment is being offered, public examining bodies would have to demonstrate that they know what it is that they are measuring by specifying the types of operation they intend to test and be able to show meaningfully in their assessment what a candidate could actually do with the language.

Morrow also points out that if the communicative point of view is adopted there would be no one overall test of language proficiency. Language would need to be taught and tested according to the specific needs of the learner; ie in terms of specified communicative criteria. Carroll (1980) makes reference to this:

> '. . . different patterns of communication will entail different configurations of language skill mastery and therefore a different course or test content.'

Through a system of profile reporting, a learner's performance could be differentially assessed in different communicative areas and the scores related to specific communicative objectives.

2 Is it a job worth doing?

Davies (1978) suggests that by the mid '70s, approaches to testing would seem to fall along a continuum which stretches from 'pure' discrete item tests at one end, to integrative tests such as cloze at the other. He takes the view that in testing, as in teaching, there is a tension between the analytical on the one hand and the integrative on the other. For Davies:

'. . . the most satisfactory view of language testing and the most useful kinds of language tests, are a combination of these two views, the analytical and the integrative.'

Morrow argues that this view pays insufficient regard to the importance of the productive and receptive processing of discourse arising out of the actual use of language in a social context with all the attendant performance constraints, eg processing in real time, unpredictability, the interaction-based nature of discourse, context, purpose and behavioural outcomes.

A similar view is taken by Kelly (1978) who puts forward a convincing argument that if the goal of applied linguistics is seen as the applied analysis of meaning, eg the recognition of the context-specific meaning of an utterance as distinct from its system-giving meaning, then we as applied linguists should be more interested in the development and measurement of ability to take part in specified communicative performance, the production of and comprehension of coherent discourse, rather than in linguistic competence. It is not, thus, a matter of whether candidates know, eg through summing the number of correct responses to a battery of discrete-point items in such restricted areas as morphology, syntax, lexis and phonology, but rather, to take the case of comprehension, whether they can use this knowledge in combination with other available evidence to recover the writer's or speaker's context-specific meaning. Morrow would seem justified in his view that if we are to assess proficiency, ie potential success in the use of the language in some general sense, it would be more valuable to test for a knowledge of and an ability to apply the rules and processes, by which these discrete elements are synthesized into an infinite number of grammatical sentences and then selected as being appropriate for a particular context, rather than simply test a knowledge of the elements alone.

In response to a feeling that discrete-point tests were in some ways inadequate indicators of language proficiency, the testing pendulum swung in favour of global tests in the 1970s, an approach to measurement that was in many ways contrary to the allegedly atomistic assumptions of the discrete-point testers. It is claimed by Oller (1979) that global integrative tests such as cloze and dictation go beyond the measurement of a limited part of language competence achieved by discrete-point tests and can measure the ability to integrate disparate language skills in ways which more closely approximate to the actual process of language use. He maintains that provided linguistic tests such as cloze require 'performance' under real life contraints, eg time, they are at least a guide to aptitude and potential for communication even if not tests of communication itself.

Kelly (1978) is not entirely satisfied by this argument and although he admits that to the extent that:

'. . . they require testees to operate at many different levels simultaneously, as in authentic communication, global tests of the indirect kind have a greater initial plausibility than discrete items . . . and certainly more than those items which are both discrete and indirect, such as multiple-choice tests of syntax.'

he argues that:

'only a direct test which simulates as closely as possible authentic communication tasks of interest to the tester can have a first order validity ie one derived from some model of communicative interaction.'

Even if it were decided that indirect tests such as cloze were valid in some sort of derived fashion, it still remains that performing on a cloze test is not the same sort of activity as reading.

This is a point taken up by Morrow who argues that indirect integrative tests, though global in that they require candidates to exhibit simultaneous control over many different aspects of the language system and often of other aspects of verbal interaction as well, do not necessarily measure the ability to communicate in a foreign language. Morrow correctly emphasises that though indirect measures of language abilities claim extremely high standards of reliability and validity as established by statistical techniques, the claim to validity remains suspect.

Morrow's advocacy of more direct, performance-based tests of actual communication has not escaped criticism though. One argument voiced is that communication is not co-terminous with language and a lot of communication is non-linguistic. In any case, the conditions for actual real-life communication are not replicable in a test situation which appears to be by necessity artificial and idealised and, to use Davies's phrase (1978), Morrow is perhaps fruitlessly pursuing 'the chimera of authenticity'.

Morrow is also understandably less than explicit with regard to the nature and extent of the behavioural outcomes we might be interested in testing and the enabling skills which contribute to their realisation. Whereas we might come nearer to specifying the latter as our knowledge of the field grows, the possibility of ever specifying 'communicative performance', of developing a grammar of language in use, is surely beyond us given the unbounded nature of the surface realisations.

Reservations must also be expressed concerning Morrow's use of the phrase 'performance tests'. A test which seeks to establish how the learner performs in a single situation, because this is the only situation in which the learner will have to use the target language, (a very unlikely state of affairs) could be considered a performance test. A performance test is a test which samples behaviours in a single setting with no intention of generalising beyond that setting. Any other type of test is bound to concern itself with competence for the very act of generalising beyond the setting actually tested implies some statement about abilities to use and/or knowledge. In view of this it would perhaps be more accurate if instead of talking in terms of testing performance ability we merely claimed to be evaluating samples of performance, in certain specific contexts of use created under particular test constraints, for what they could tell us about a candidate's underlying competence.

Though a knowledge of the elements of a language might well be a necessary prerequisite to language use, it is difficult to see how any extension of a structuralist language framework could accommodate the testing of communicative skills in the sense Morrow is using the term. Further, a framework such as Lado's might allow us to infer a student's knowledge which might be adequate, perhaps, for diagnostic/ordering purposes, but is it adequate for predicting the ability of a student to use language in any communicative situation?

I do not feel we are yet in a position to give any definite answer to the question 'Is communicative testing a job worth doing?'. Though I would accept that linguistic competence must be an essential part of communicative competence, the way in which they relate to each other or either relates to communicative performance has in no sense been clearly established by empirical research. There is a good deal of work that needs to be done in comparing results obtained from linguistically based tests with those which sample communicative performance before one can make any positive statements about the former being a sufficient indication of likely ability in the latter or in real-life situations.

Before any realistic comparisons are possible, reliable, effective, as well as valid, methods for **establishing** and **testing** relevant communicative tasks and enabling skills need to be devised and investigated. This raises the last of the three questions posed at the start of this paper: 'How feasible is communicative testing?'. A satisfactory standard of test reliability is essential because communicative tests, to be considered valid, must first be proven reliable. Rea (1978) argues that simply because tests which assess language as communication cannot automatically claim high standards of reliability in the same way that discrete item tests are able to, this should not be accepted as a justification for continued reliance on measures with very suspect validity.

Rather, we should first be attempting to obtain more reliable measures of communicative abilities if we are to make sensible statements about their feasibility.

3 Is it feasible?

Corder (1973) noted:

> 'The more ambitious we are in testing the communicative competence of a learner, the more administratively costly, subjective and unreliable the results are.'

Because communicative tests will involve us to a far greater extent in the assessment of actual written and oral communication, doubts have been expressed concerning time, expenditure, ease of construction, scoring, requirements in terms of skilled manpower and equipment, in fact, about the practicability of a communicative test in all its manifestations. To add to these problems we still lack a systematic description of the language code in use in meaningful situations and a comprehensive account of language as a system of communication.

For Kelly (1978) the possibility of devising a construct-valid proficiency test, ie one that measures ability to communicate in the target language, is dependent on the prior existence of:

> '. . . appropriate objectives for the test to measure.'

Advocates of communicative tests seem to be arguing that it is only necessary to select certain representative communication tasks as we do not use the same language for all possible communication purposes. In the case of proficiency tests, these tasks are seen as inherent in the nature of the communication situation for which candidates are being assessed. Caution, however, would demand that we wait until empirical evidence is available before making such confident statements concerning the identification of these tasks as only by first examining the feasibility of establishing suitable objectives through research into real people coping with real situations, will we have any basis for investigating the claims that might be made for selecting a representative sample of operational tasks to assess performance ability. Even if it were possible to establish suitable objectives, ie successfully identify tasks and underlying constituent enabling skills, then we would still have to meet the further criticism that the more authentic the language task we test, the more difficult it is to measure reliably. If, as Morrow suggests, we seek to construct simulated communication tasks which closely resemble those a candidate would face in real life and which make realistic demands on him in terms of language performance behaviours, then we will certainly encounter problems especially in the areas of extrapolation and assessment.

Kelly (1978) observed that any kind of test is an exercise in sampling and from this sample an attempt is made to infer students' capabilities in relation to their performance in general:

> 'That is, of all that a student is expected to know and/or do as a result of his course of study (in an achievement test) or that the position requires (in the case of a proficiency test), a test measures students only on a selected sample. The reliability of a test in this conception is the extent to which the score on the test is a stable indication of candidates' ability in relation to the wider universe of knowledge, performance, etc., that are of interest.'

He points out that even if there is available a clear set of communication tasks:

> '. . . the number of different communication problems a candidate will have to solve in the real world conditions is as great as the permutations and combinations produced by the values of the variables in the sorts of messages, contexts of situation and performance conditions that may be encountered.'

Thus on the basis of performance, on a particular item, one ought to be circumspect, to say the least, in drawing conclusions about a candidate's ability to handle similar communication tasks.

In order to make stable predictions of student performance in relation to the indefinitely large universe of tasks, it thus seems necessary to sample candidates' performances on as large a number of tasks as is possible, which conflicts immediately with the demands of test efficiency. The larger the sample, and the more realistic the test items, the longer the test will have to be.

In the case of conventional language tests aimed at measuring mastery of the language code, extrapolation would seem to pose few problems. The grammatical and phonological systems of a language are finite and manageable and the lexical resources can be delimited. The infinite number of sentences in a language are made up of a finite number of elements and thus tests of the mastery of these elements are extremely powerful from a predictive point of view. Thus, we might tend to agree with Davies (1978):

'. . . what remains a convincing argument in favour of linguistic competence tests (both discrete point and integrative) is that grammar is at the core of language learning . . . Grammar is far more powerful in terms of generalisability than any other language feature.'

However, Kelly (1978) puts forward an interesting argument against this viewpoint. It is not known, for example, how crucial a complete mastery of English verb morphology is to the overall objective of being able to communicate in English, or how serious a disability it is not to know the second conditional. We thus have:

'. . . no reliable knowledge of the relative functional importance of the various structures in a language.'

Given this failing, it would seem impossible to make any claims about what students should be able to do in a language on the basis of scores on a discrete-point test of syntax. The construct, ability to communicate in the language, involves more than a mere manipulation of certain syntactic patterns with a certain lexical content. In consequence, it seems we still need to devise measuring instruments which can assess communicative ability in some more meaningful way.

As a way out of the extrapolation quandary, Kelly (1978) suggests a two-stage approach to the task of devising a test that represents a possible compromise between the conflicting demands of the criteria of validity, reliability and efficiency.

'The first stage involves the development of a direct test that is maximally valid and reliable, and hence inefficient. The second stage calls for the development of efficient, hence indirect, tests of high validity. The validity of the indirect tests is to be determined by reference to the first battery of direct tasks.'

As far as large-scale proficiency testing is concerned, another suggestion that has been made is that we should focus attention on language use in individual and specified situations while retaining, for purposes of extrapolation, tests of the candidate's ability to handle that aspect of language which obviously is generalisable to all language use situations, namely the grammatical and phonological systems. The hard line Morrow has adopted in the article under consideration makes it unlikely that he would contemplate either of these suggestions and would continue to argue for the use of pure direct performance-based tests.

Morrow's argument is that a model (as yet unrealised) for the performance of global communicative tasks may show, for any task, the enabling skills which have to be mobilised to complete it. He argues that assessment of ability in using these skills would yield data which are relevant across a broad spectrum of global tasks, and are not limited to a single instance of performance, though in practice these are by no means as easy to specify as precisely as he assumes nor are there any guidelines available for assessing their relative importance for the successful completion of a particular communicative operation, let alone their relative weighting across a spectrum of tasks. He is also aware that there exists in tests of enabling skills a fundamental weakness in the relationship between the whole and the parts, as a candidate may prove quite capable of handling individual enabling skills and be incapable of mobilising them in a use situation or developing appropriate strategies to communicate effectively.

In practice it is by no means easy even to identify those enabling skills which might be said together to contribute towards the successful completion of a communicative task. Morrow would appear to assume that we are not only able to establish these enabling skills, but also able to describe the relationship that exists between the part and the whole in a fairly accurate manner (in this case, how 'separate' enabling skills contribute to the communicative task). He would seem to assume that there is a prescribed formula:

$$\frac{\text{possession and use of}}{\text{enabling skills X+Y+Z}} = \frac{\text{successful completion of}}{\text{communicative task}}$$

whereas it would seem likely that the added presence of a further skill or the absence of a named skill might still result in successful completion of the task in hand.

The second main problem area for Morrow is that of assessment. Given that performance is an integrated phenomenon, a quantitative assessment procedure would seem to be invalid so some form of qualitative assessment must be found. This has obvious implications for reliability. A criticism often made is that it is not possible to assess production qualitatively in ways which are not hopelessly subjective. For Morrow, the answer seems to lie in the concept of an operational scale of attainment, in which different levels of proficiency are defined in terms of a set of performance criteria. B J Carroll (op. cit. and 1978a and this volume) distinguishes different levels of perform-ance by matching the candidate's performance with operational specifications which take account of parameters such as:

size, complexity, range, speed, flexibility, accuracy, appropriacy, independence, repetition and hesitation.

Morrow, as Carroll, advocates the use of a qualitative-synthetic approach, a form of banded mark scheme (see Caroll, this volume, for examples of this type of rating scheme) where an overall impression mark is awarded on the basis of specified criteria in preference to any analytic scheme. It is quite likely that the operational parameters of B J Carroll (op. cit.) eg size, complexity, range, accuracy, appropriacy, etc., will be subject to amendment in practice and in some cases even omission, but as Morrow argues in the article under review:

'. . . they seem to offer a way of assessing the quality of performance at different levels in a way which combines face validity with at least potential reliability.'

There are no published data on the degree of marker reliability which can be achieved using a scheme of this sort, but Morrow's experience with the new R S A examination and the vast experience of G C E boards in the impression-based marking of essays suggests that standardisation meetings should enable **fairly** consistent scorings to be achieved, or at least as consistent as those achieved by analytical marking procedures.

Perhaps the point that should be made in answer to the question 'Is it feasible?' is that once again we do not yet know the answer. Until we have actually sought to confront the problems in practice, I feel it would be wrong to condemn communicative testing out of hand. What is needed is empirical research into the feasibility of establishing communicative tests, plus a comparison of the results that can be obtained through these procedures with those that are provided by discrete-point and indirect integrative measures.

BIBLIOGRAPHY

CANALE, M and SWAIN, M
Theoretical bases of communicative approaches to second language teaching and testing. In: Journal of applied linguistics, 1, 1, 1-47, 1980.

CARROLL, B J
An English language testing service: specifications. London: British Council, 1978 and this volume.

CARROLL, B J
Guidelines for the development of communicative tests. London: Royal Society of Arts, 1978a.

CARROLL, B J
Testing communicative performance: an interim study. Pergamon, 1980.

COOPER, R L
An elaborated testing model. In: Language learning (special issue) 3: Problems in foreign language testing, 57-72, 1968.

CORDER, S P
Introducing applied linguistics. London: Penguin, 1973.

DAVIES, A ed.
Language testing symposium: a psycholinguistic approach. London: Oxford University Press, 1968.

DAVIES, A
Language testing: survey article. In: Language teaching and linguistics abstracts, 2 3/4; part 1: 145-159; part 2: 215-231; 1978.

FITZPATRICK, R and MORRISON, E J
Performance and product evaluation. In: THORNDIKE, R L, ed. Educational measurement. 2nd ed. Washington, DG: American Council on Education, 1971.

HYMES, D H
On communicative competence. In: PRIDE AND HOLMES, eds, Sociolinguistics. Harmondsworth: Penguin, 1972, pp 269-293 (excerpts from the paper published 1971 by University of Pennsylvania Press, Philadelphia).

KELLY, R
On the construct validation of comprehension tests: an exercise in applied linguistics. PhD. University of Queensland, 1978.

MORROW, K
Techniques of evaluation for a notional syllabus. London: Royal Society of Arts, 1977.

MORROW, K
Testing: revolution or evolution. In: JOHNSON, K and BRUMFIT, C, eds. The communicative approach to language teaching. London: Oxford University Press, 1979 and this volume.

OLLER, J W
Language tests at school. London: Longman, 1979.

REA, P M
Assessing language as communication. In: MALS journal (new series: 3). University of Birmingham: Department of English, 1978.

ROYAL SOCIETY OF ARTS
Examinations in the communicative use of English as a foreign language: specifications and specimen papers. London: Royal Society of Arts, 1980.

SPOLSKY, B
Language testing: the problem of validation. In: TESOL quarterly, 2, 88-94, 1968.

WIDDOWSON, H G
Teaching language as communication. London: Oxford University Press, 1978.

REACTION TO THE MORROW PAPER (2)
Alan Moller, The British Council, London

Morrow's article is an important contribution to the discussion of communicative language testing. Some of the content, however, is marred by a somewhat emotional tone, although Morrow admits at the end that the title is rhetorical. The effect on the reader who is not informed about language testing could be misleading. The case for communicative language testing may well be stated forthrightly and with conviction, but talk of 'revolution' and 'spilling of blood' implies a crusading spirit which is not appropriate. The most traditional forms of language examining, and indeed of examining in most subjects, have been the viva and the dissertation or essay, both basic forms of communication. Reintroduction of these forms of examining, with some modifications, can hardly be termed revolutionary. What is new is the organisation of these traditional tasks. The nature of the task is more clearly specified, there is a more rigorous approach to the assessing of the language produced, and the label given to this process is new. More suitable titles for this discussion might be 'language testing: the communicative dimension', or 'communicative language testing: a re-awakening'.

Work in this area is recent and falls within the compass of what Spolsky (1975) termed the psycholinguistic-sociolinguistic phase of language testing. However, it is perhaps time to identify a fourth phase in language testing, closely linked to the third, the sociolinguistic-communicative phase.

As is often the case with discussion of communicative competence, communicative performance, and now communicative testing, no definition is given! But the characteristics identified by Morrow give some indication as to what might be included in definitions. It would seem that the general purpose of communicative tests is to establish first whether communication is taking place and secondly the degree of acceptability of the communication. This implies making judgements on the effectiveness and the quality of the communication observed.

The deficiencies of the structuralist method of language teaching and of that phase of language testing are well rehearsed, and Morrow need not have devoted so much space to it. He was right to point out J B Carroll's (1968) underlining of the integrated skills of listening, speaking, reading and writing.

But he has failed to point out that although integrated texts were presented to students, and although students were often asked to produce short integrated texts, the items themselves were normally discrete, focusing on structural or lexical features. While agreeing that the primacy of contrastive analysis as a basis of language tests is no longer acceptable, we must beware of implying or insisting that the primacy of language as communication is the sole basis for language proficiency tests.

Discussions on language testing normally touch on two key questions. Morrow's concern with language as communication and his failure to define communicative language testing ensure that reaction to his article bring these questions to the fore:

1 What is language, and what is language performance?
2 What is to be tested?

In answer to these questions we might propose the following definition of communicative language testing:

an assessment of the ability to use one or more of the phonological, syntactic and semantic systems of the language

1 so as to communicate ideas and information to another speaker/reader in such a way that the intended meaning of the message communicated is received and understood, and

2 so as to receive and understand the meaning of a message communicated by another speaker/writer that the speaker/writer intended to convey.

This assessment will involve judging the quality of the message, the quality of the expression and of its transmission, and the quality of its reception in its transmission.

Morrow has commented on discrete item (atomistic) tests and integrated (competence) tests and concluded that neither type 'gives any convincing proof of the candidate's ability to actually use the language'. Seven features of language use 'which do not seem to be measured in conventional tests' are then examined. If by conventional tests is meant discrete item and integrated tests, it is true that certain features may not be measured. It is equally questionable whether some of these features are even measured in so-called communicative tests. Does the measurement of a subject's performance include measuring the purpose of the text, its authenticity or its unpredictability, for example? It would seem to me that the claim is being made that these features are not present in the test task in conventional tests. Even this claim is not entirely accurate.

It is helpful to examine the characteristics put forward by Morrow individually. **Purpose of text** The implication that every utterance produced in a communicative test is purposeful may not always be so. In many tests candidates may participate in communication and make statements which fulfil no other purpose than to follow the rules of what is likely to be an artificial situation. There is apparent purpose to the text being uttered, but the text may genuinely be no more purposeful than the texts presented in discrete and integrative test tasks. **Context** There are few items, even in discrete item tests, that are devoid of context. Communicative tests may attempt to make the context more plausible. **Performance** is not wholly absent from integrative tests, although it may be limited. Perhaps what is meant is production. **Interaction** Many conventional reading and listening tests are not based on interaction between the candidate and another speaker/hearer, but the candidate does **interact** with the text both in cloze and dictation. **Authenticity** This notion has been questioned elsewhere by Davies (1980) and seems to me to need careful definition. Language generated in a communicative test may be authentic only insofar as it is authentic to the context of a language test. It may be no more authentic — in the sense of resembling real life communication outside the test room — than many a reading comprehension passage. **Unpredictability** It is certain that unpredictability can occur naturally and can be built into tests of oral interaction. This feature would seem to be accounted for most satisfactorily in communicative language tests as would certain **behaviour** as the outcome of communicative test tasks.

Thus there are only two features of language use which are likely to occur only in communicative language tests. The absence or presence of seven characteristics in different types of test is shown more clearly in the table below. Column D refers to discrete item testing, column I to integrative tests and column C to communicative tests. Absence of a characteristic is indicated by X and presence by √.

There is, however, an important difference in the role of the candidate in the various kinds of tests. In the discrete and integrative tests the candidate is an **outsider.** The text of the test is imposed on him. He has to respond and interact in the ways set down. But in communicative performance tests the candidate is an **insider,** acting in and shaping the communication, producing the text together with the person with whom he is interacting.

Characteristics	D	I	C
Purpose of text	x	✓	✓
Context	(✓)	✓	✓
Performance	x	✓(limited)	✓
Interaction	x	✓	✓
Authenticity	?	?	?
Unpredictability	x	x	✓
Behaviour-based	x	x	✓

There may be little new in the subject's actual performance in communicative language tests. The main differences between traditional (pre-scientific) and communicative tests will lie more in the content of the tests and the way in which student performance is assessed. The content of the tests will be specified in terms of linguistic tasks and not in terms of linguistic items. Tests will be constructed in accordance with specifications and not simply to conform to formats of previous tests. Criteria for assessment will also be specified to replace simple numerical or grading scales which frequently do not make it clear what the points on the scale stand for. Certain criteria at different levels of performance will be worked out incorporating agreed parameters. These criteria may well take the form of a set of descriptions.

Another way of comparing communicative language testing with other types of tests is by considering the relative importance of the roles of the test constructor, the subject (or candidate) and the assessor in each of the phases of language testing identified by Spolsky — the pre-scientific, the psychometric-structuralist, and the psycholinguistic-sociolinguistic (competence) phases. The table below summarises these roles. The type of test is given on the left, column T refers to the role of the test constructor, column S to the role of the student, and column A to the role of the assessor. A √ indicates the importance of the role, (√) indicates minor importance, and (   ) no importance.

Test type	T	S	A
Pre-scientific	(√)	√	√
Psych/Struct	√	(√)	( )
Psych/Socio	(√)	√	(√)
Communicative	√	√	√

This table suggests that whereas in the pre-scientific and psycholinguistic/ sociolinguistic (competence) tests the role of the test constructor (T) in setting questions and choosing texts is not important in the sense of being neither arduous, complex nor lengthy, his role is much more dominant in the psychometric/structuralist tests and communicative tests. In the psychometric/structuralist tests the work of the test constructor is all important, the task of the subject (S) is essentially to recognise or select, and in the majority of tests of this type marking is objective with therefore no role for the assessor (A). In the psycholinguistic/sociolinguistic tests, as defined, the main role is assumed by the subject who interacts with the text in his task of restoring it to its original or to an acceptable form. Communicative tests, however, are exacting at all stages, and the test constructor may well participate in the oral interaction with the subject and seek to introduce new tasks or different features of language use during the live interaction. His main preoccupations will be to set performance (global) tasks that will incorporate the language skills, microskills (enabling skills) and content that have been specified in order to provoke the subject to generate appropriate communication. The subject will seek to impress the assessor by carrying out the communication effectively and by responding to unpredictable shifts in the communication, and to new topics and new tasks. The assessor is confronted with communication that is unpredictable and of varying quality on which he must impose his pre-determined scale of criteria and reach a conclusion.

Morrow is right to point out that communicative language performance will be criterion-referenced as opposed to norm-referenced. The definition of these criteria is one of the major factors in the establishment of the validity of such tests. The relevance and consistency of these criteria are crucial and lead naturally to the question of the reliability of such tests.

It will be seen from the above table that communicative tests, in common with pre-scientific tests, put a lot of responsibility on the assessor in the testing process. The subjectivity of the assessment gives rise to the problem of the reliability of such tests. Morrow touches on this problem, but it is not sufficient to say that it will simply be subordinate to face validity. Some further statement needs to be made. Careful specification of the tasks to be performed and careful specification of criteria for assessment are essential steps in the process of reducing the unreliability of this type of test. In the final analysis it may well be necessary to accept lower than normally accepted levels of reliability.

It has not been the intention of this reaction to Morrow's paper to consider in detail the points he has made but rather to use many of his observations as points of departure in an attempt to establish what communicative language performance might be, what it is that is being tested, and how valid assessments might be arrived at. It has been suggested that communicative language performance relates to the transmission and understanding of particular meanings in particular contexts and that what is being tested is the quality and effectiveness of the performance observed. Since this performance is highly subjective on the part of the subject and since the assessment must also be subjective, the reliability and validity of such tests will not be easy to establish. Careful specification of test tasks and assessment criteria would seem to be essential, but comparisons with other forms of language testing suggest that communicative testing places a heavier burden on test constructor, candidate and assessor. This does not mean that achievement of valid tests is impossible but implies more careful training of constructors and assessors and close monitoring of all phases of the testing process. Experience with ELTS [1] to date supports this contention.

There is a tendency when discussing new developments in language teaching and testing to throw out previous 'orthodoxies' and replace them with the latest one. Morrow's article has repeated the observation that good performance on a large number of discrete items in structuralist tests does not necessarily add up to ability to integrate them in effective language use. In discussing enabling skills the same problem of relating the parts to the whole has been observed. Communicative language testing seems to me to be primarily concerned with presenting subjects with integrated texts with which to interact, and with presenting them with sets of integrated tasks which will lead them to produce integrated spoken or written 'text'. As such the focus would seem to be predominantly on the whole rather than on the parts.

---

[1] English Language Testing Service administered jointly by the British Council and the University of Cambridge Local Examinations Syndicate.

Morrow suggests that the purpose of communicative testing may be proficiency testing. Later he suggests that proficiency tests will be specified in terms of communicative criteria. It is clear that communicative testing does test certain aspects of proficiency. But it is important to be aware that testing language proficiency does not amount just to communicative testing. Communicative language performance is clearly an element in, or a dimension of, language proficiency. But language competence is also an important dimension of language proficiency and cannot be ignored. It will also have to be tested in one or more of the many ways that have been researched during the past 30 years. Ignoring this dimension is as serious an omission as ignoring the re-awakening of traditional language testing in a communicative setting. Communicative language testing need not mean spilling the rather thin blood of present day language testing but could even enrich it!

BIBLIOGRAPHY

CARROLL, J B
  The psychology of language testing. In: DAVIES, A, ed. Language testing symposium: a psycholinguistic approach. London: Oxford University Press, 1968.

DAVIES, A
  John Oller and the restoration of the test. Paper presented at the Second International IUS Symposium, Darmstadt, May 1980.

SPOLSKY, B
  Language testing: art or science? Paper presented at the Fourth AILA International Congress, Stuttgart, 1975.

REACTION TO THE MORROW PAPER (3)
J Charles Alderson, University of Lancaster

One of the main problems I seem to have with this paper is that I am not sure what it is about. The title implies a discussion of the issue of whether communicative language testing is fundamentally different from 'traditional' language testing, and the conclusion suggests the same when it says that the differences between the two approaches are really quite considerable. However, I agree with Morrow himself that this hardly matters: what would seem to be important is the precise nature of these differences and in particular the precise nature of communicative language tests. I am not sure that the paper does this, or even sets out to do so. The paper fails to identify traditional language tests despite frequent reference to them. Of course, an unknown or unidentified bogeyman is easy to attack, since the truth or accuracy of the attack cannot be ascertained. This is the not unfamiliar straw man syndrome. However, this opposition between traditional and communicative tests may not be the theme of the paper, since Morrow states 'this paper will be concerned with the implications for test design and construction of the desire to measure communicative proficiency' and later it is claimed that the paper has outlined 'some of the characteristics of language in use as communication which existing tests fail to measure or to take account of in a systematic way' and will examine 'some of the implications of building them into the design specification for language tests'. Note that 'existing tests' are not identified, so that it is difficult to evaluate the claim. The second footnote of the paper leads one to expect that criteria will be established for the design of communicative tests, by its criticism of the ARELS and JMB tests for not meeting 'in a rigorous way' such criteria. Unfortunately, this most interesting area remains undeveloped, since it is never clear what the criteria for the construction of communicative tests are, or how the JMB and ARELS tests fail to meet such criteria. Morrow goes on to say that working parties have been established to 'assess the feasibility of tests based on communicative criteria' but tantalisingly does not specify what these criteria are or might be. I wonder whether this is not the basic problem with the paper, namely that criteria are promised but not established. The importance of such criteria is that they would allow one not only to attempt to construct communicative language tests, but also to judge the feasibility or success of such attempts. Although the article goes on to talk about 'features of language use', 'characteristics of a test of communicative ability' and 'answers to questions', none of these amounts to an explicit statement of criteria, although, conceivably, such might be derived by implication from the criticisms of 'traditional' language tests. And indeed, later on we do appear to be back with the apparent topic of the paper, 'the central distinction between what has gone before and what is now being proposed' and this is stated as being 'the relationship between performance and the way it is achieved and the testing strategy which it is legitimate to adopt in order to measure it'. My confusion may stem from two sources: the already mentioned failure of Morrow's clearly to identify exactly which tests are being attacked as 'traditional', allied with a failure to define terms like 'communicative proficiency', 'language competence', 'performance test', 'behavioural outcome', and so on; and on the other hand, my feeling that it is not necessary to draw unsubstantiated and inevitably over-simplified distinctions between past and present practice in language testing in order to explore the important issue of how to test communicative proficiency however that might be defined. It is, I think, important to bear in mind that Morrow is probably talking about proficiency testing — tests designed by examination bodies, or for organisations like the British Council — rather than about classroom tests. It is unlikely that the latter have been consistently guilty of placing too much importance on reliability, or accepting 'validity of a statistical rather than a practical nature', or of confining itself to 'the directly quantifiable modes of assessment', as he suggests. But even within the confines of proficiency testing, I fear Morrow overstates his case. He claims, for example, that the traditional 'measurement of language proficiency depends crucially on the assumption that (language) proficiency is neatly quantifiable in this way' (ie atomistically). I wonder whether traditional language testing 'crucially' depends on this assumption, in which case one might very well reject it, or whether the fact is not something more sensible, namely that such quantification is actually possible, unlike other, perhaps more direct and indeed desirable 'measurements' and that such quantitative measures at least give some indications, in an indirect manner, of some aspect of language proficiency. It seems that such an interpretation would not then rule out the value of qualitative measurement, even within traditional testing theory. The same point recurs when Morrow claims that an atomistic approach depends utterly on the assumption that knowledge of the parts equals knowledge of the whole. Do we know or believe that such is the assumption (in which case, Morrow is probably correct) or do we believe that the traditional testing position is one of assuming that we can infer the knowledge of the whole from the knowledge of the parts? Perhaps this is another example of the straw man syndrome. Similarly with the analogy with car driving which, although commonplace, is actually misleading. Nobody would wish to claim that a knowledge of the isolated elements of the integrated skill is sufficient for use, just as nobody would wish to claim that knowing how to manipulate the throttle, brake, clutch and so on of a car amounts to driving a car. The real issue is whether such knowledge, and in particular the knowledge of words, and of structure is necessary, and if necessary whether such knowledge is precisely specifiable and therefore testable. Even Carroll's 'clear statement of an "integrated" position' recognises the need for both integration **and** atomism: one cannot interpret his (oft-quoted) remarks to mean that Carroll was against atomism merely because on its own he felt it to be insufficient. Morrow wishes to add the 'ability to synthesise'' to the ability to analyse language, but it seems important to examine in more detail precisely what such an ability is. Leaving aside conceivably equally important factors like the ability to operate under pressure of time, emotion, society and the like, the synthetic ability would seem worthy of much more treatment than it gets from Morrow in this paper. The nature or indeed existence of enabling skills, which we look at in more detail later, would perhaps qualify as part of such an examination.

Another charge levelled against (unidentified) traditional testing is that it views language learning as a 'process of accretion'. Now, if this were true, one would probably wish to condemn such an aberration, but is it? Does it follow from an atomistic approach to language that one views the **process** of learning as an accretion? This does not necessarily follow from the notion that the **product** of language learning is a series of items (among other things). Be that as it may, the alternative view of language learning that Morrow presents is not in fact an alternative, since by the same reasoning inter-languages can be acquired through accretion. No different view of the language learning process is necessarily implied, as far as I can see, by the notion of inter-language, which can be translated as one or more intermediate products on the road to proficiency.

Incidentally, contrary to what Morrow states, a 'structural/contrastive analysis' does not appear to follow necessarily from an atomistic approach although it is probably impossible without such an approach. It does not make sense to rule out contrastive analysis as the background for, or one of the inputs to, all test construction: presumably its usefulness depends on the test's purpose, and contrastive analysis may very well be useful for diagnostic tests.

Morrow's coyness when it comes to identifying actual examples of traditional testing, makes it extremely difficult to evaluate his claims, particularly for communicative language testing. In particular, he claims that there are seven features of language use that are not taken account of in 'conventional tests'. Now these features of language use are undeniable, and it is helpful to have them listed in this paper, but I doubt very much whether 'conventional tests' do not measure them. Of course, the question of how one knows or establishes whether they do or do not is of central importance, both for traditional tests and for communicative tests, since the issue is one of validation. If one uses the same technique that Morrow himself employs in the discussion of cloze and dictation, (that is, face validity) then it is almost certainly just not true that conventional tests took no account of unpredictability, interaction, context, purpose, performance and so on. Of course, the crucial question, whatever the historical truth, is how will the 'new types of test' take account of these seven features 'systematically'? The question is evaded, as is the issue of the exhaustiveness of the list: ought we not perhaps consider an extension of the list of features to account more fully for the nature of language use, and include other features like deviance, and negotiated meaning, or the frequent existence of mutually conflicting interpretations of communicative interactions, and then examine the consequences in testing terms of such a list?

The assertion that conventional tests fail to account for the seven features of language use is not the only unsubstantiated claim that is made in the paper, and some of the claims seem central to the argument. 'The demand for context-free language production fails to measure the extent to which features of the candidate's performance may in fact hamper communication' — the fact is that we simply do not know whether this is true or not, or indeed, how to investigate it: what criteria shall we use to measure the hampering of communication? Traditional tests are criticised implicitly for using simplified texts rather than 'authentic' texts and tasks, yet the statement that 'the ability of the candidate to, eg read a simplified text tells nothing about his actual communicative ability', is merely an assertion, and will remain as such until we can measure 'actual communicative ability', by which time, of course, we would presumably not dream of asking someone to read a simplified text instead of being directly measured for his communicative ability. (A related point is whether simplification actually makes processing easier, which Morrow appears to think it does. The evidence is at best ambiguous).

The demand for 'authenticity' is itself not unproblematic. What are 'authentic language tasks ' in a language test? Does not the very fact that the setting is one of assessment disauthenticate most 'language tests'? Are there not some language tasks which are authentic in a language test, which would be inauthentic outside that domain? I find the authenticity argument somewhat sterile since it seems to assume that the domains of language teaching and language testing do not have their own set of specifications for authentic language use which are distinct from the specifications of other domains. Thus 'What is this? — It's a pencil' is authentic language teaching language, and so on. If one does not accept this, then authentic tasks are in principle impossible in a language testing situation, and communicative language testing is in principle impossible. A related problem, possibly caused by lack of definitions results from Morrow's statement that 'the success or failure of an interaction is judged by its participants on the basis of behavioural outcomes. Strictly speaking, no other criteria are relevant'. Without a definition of behavioural outcomes, this is hard to evaluate, but on the face of things, I can only assume that this refers to certain limited language functions like the directive function. How can phatic or poetic uses of language be judged on behavioural outcomes? And why should behaviour on a language test be judged only in those terms? This presumably relates to the notion of performance test, but this term also remains undefined: what are the essential characteristics of a performance test? How is such a test to be validated? Against what? Behavioural outcomes? What would a performance test of listening look like that is different from the sorts of tests we already have? What, incidentally, would a nonintegrated test of listening be?

The question of test validation is central to any discussion of (proficiency) testing. In communicative tests, the main means of validation would appear to be content or construct validation, but without clear specification of the constructs, this is just not possible. A good example of the problems faced by the theory, and practice, is the issue of enabling skills. The paper implies that we already know the relation of such skills to performances ('An analysis of the global tasks in terms of which the candidate is to be assessed . . . will usually yield a fairly consistent set of enabling skills'), but in fact we know very little of the contribution made to any particular event by any one skill or even set of skills, and very little of the way in which such 'enabling skills' can be said to 'enable'. Even if we knew that such enabling skills existed, we would presumably need to know their relative importance overall, or even in one global task. And even if we knew this, we would still be faced with the likelihood that any one individual can plausibly do without (ie not call upon or not master) one, or a range, of the enabling skills, and still perform the task adequately: this supposition is at least as reasonable as the one that Morrow makes, and subject to the same requirement of verification. How either assertion might be verified is central to the problem of validation, and no solution appears obvious. The same point would appear to apply to the parameters of B J Carroll: to what extent, if at all, are the actual values of these parameters of size, range, accuracy, appropriacy and the like, actually specifiable for any one communicative event? If the values are not specifiable in terms of some notion of the ideal performance (a requirement of criterion-reference testing, which is what Morrow claims— and it remains a claim — communicative testing to be) then what is the use of such parameters? The question is complicated by this notion of the ideal (or optimal) performance: whose performance, which performance is criterial? Morrow implies in the paper that we are to compare non-native speakers' performance with those of native speakers ('Tests of receptive skills will similarly be concerned with revealing the extent to which the candidate's processing abilities match those of a native speaker'). How are we to compare the performance of the two groups (natives and non-natives)? Which native speakers are we to take? Are all native speakers to be assumed to be able to perform ideally on communicative tests? We know native speakers differ in at least some communicative abilities (reading, oracy, fluency) — how can they be compared with non-natives? This aspect of the criteria question is simply ignored: how are we to judge performances on our tests? Tests, after all, are not merely elicitation devices for getting at samples of language behaviour, but assessment procedures: 'Tests will, thus, be concerned with making the learner produce samples of his own interlanguage based on his own norms of language production so that conclusions can be drawn from it' (Morrow, this volume p. 12). What sort of conclusions will be drawn and why? The questions are not asked.

How are we to evaluate communicative language tests? What criteria are we to use to help us construct them, or to help us determine their validity? It has been suggested that Morrow does not provide us with any explicit statements on this. However, some criteria are surely possible, unrelated to any particular view of language or language use in the sense of being determined by such a view; the criteria are statable in the form of questions one might pose of a test: in a sense they are meta-criteria, and the validity of the answers depends on the validity of the related theories. The questions one should ask of language tests (of any sort, not only proficiency tests), when judging them, when discussing the issue of test validity — does the test measure what it claims to measure? — can be divided into four areas: the test's view of language, the test's view of the learner, the test's view of learning and background knowledge:

What is the test's view of language?

What is 'knowing a language' in the test's terms?
Does the test view language as a set of isolated, separable items?
Does performance on the test reflect performance in the real world?
Do the testees have to **do** things with language?
Does the test measure the ability to function within a specified set of sociolinguistic domains?
Is the test based on a model of communication?
Does the test relate to the sociolinguistic variables that affect the use of language in communication?
(eg Does the test measure the learner's ability to recognise the effect of, and produce appropriate language for:
     the setting of a communication?
     the topic of a communication?
     the function of a communication?
     the modality of a communication?
     the presuppositions in a communication?
     the degree of formality of a communication?
     the roles of participants in a communication?

the status of participants in a communication?
the attitudes of participants in a communication?)

Does the test take account of the fact that communication:
is interaction-based?
is unpredictable?
takes place under pressure of time?
takes place in a context?
takes place for a purpose?
is behaviour-based?
is not necessarily totally dependent on language?
that is,
are student reactions predictable?
are complex language skills measured?
is the situation real?
is the ability to **interpret** original messages measured?
is the ability to **produce** original messages measured?
is the **creative** element of language use tapped?
is the testee's **participation** required?

What is 'meaning' according to the test?
static, residing in words?
variable, according to context?
negotiable, depending on all the factors in the interaction?
Does the test recognise that language is redundant?
Is the language sample of the test biassed?, ie inauthentic, unusual.
Does the test cover **relevant** aspects of language skills?

What is the test's view of the learner?

Does the test confine itself to the lower part of a hierarchy of skills?
Does the test make demands on the cognitive skills (knowledge of the world, understanding, reasoning)?
Does the test involve the affects of the learner especially as in interpersonal behaviour?
Is the test appropriate for the proposed testees in terms of their knowledge, affects, skills?
Does the test take account of the learner's expectations?
ie   his definition of his needs?
his notion of what it is to know a language?
Does the test allow different types of learners to show their abilities equally, or is it biassed in favour of one type of learner?
How would native speakers perform on the test?

What is the test's view of language learning?

Does the test assume that language learning is equivalent to gaining control over linguistic problems?
Is the test congruent with the aims and practices of the language teaching?
ie   is the language being tested in the way it is taught?
    are the tests appropriate both to the target performance of the course
      and to the competence which is assumed/known to underlie or enable
      that performance?
    is the weighting (balance) of subtests appropriate to the language
    teaching?

Background knowledge?

Are extraneous variables — culture, subject-specific knowledge — involved in the test? Can they be excluded?
Does the test favour one type of knowledge?
Should the test have 'neutral' content? Is this possible?
Can content be separated from language?
What if the learner knows what to say, but does not know how to say it?
If we are to measure communication, which includes **ideational** knowledge, then should not the subject specialist also be involved in a 'language' test?

Many of these questions derive from Morrow himself although they are not confined to this source. In a sense, they form the unspoken criteria promised but not given in this paper. The paper is really about the relationship between theories of language, language use and language learning, and tests of language knowledge, language proficiency and language use. Morrow's final set of five questions can be seen as pointing the way to such detailed questions as above. The paper and in particular this final set of five questions, is very useful for the way in which directions are suggested for future research. Indeed, the only way in which we will ever get answers to the questions posed by Morrow is by carrying out research, and for a considerable period.

Summary

It seems to me that the Morrow article contains many important points.

1 It correctly emphasises the need for testing to catch up with language teaching.

2 It implicitly suggests ways in which testing might help teaching, through the specification of language use, for example. One of the advantages of a 'testing approach' is that it forces explicitness.

3 Morrow is right to avoid continua and clines, and to argue polemically. To say that everything is really part of the same thing appears to me to be unhelpful: what is interesting is where the differences lie. Thus it is helpful to set up dichotomies, provided, naturally, that the part of the dichotomy one is putting forward is not merely a negative attack on straw men.

4 The view of language use that Morrow puts forward seems to be essentially correct, and fruitful of further hypotheses and research. He may, however, rather underestimate the **dynamic** and negotiated nature of communication.

5 He is correct to see tests as embodiments of theories, or views, of the nature of language and of language learning. This aspect of test design seems to be neglected elsewhere. As he points out, if the theory is wrong, then the validity of the test is zero.

6 The problem and importance of extrapolation and assessment are rightly stressed.

7 On the whole, he is right to criticise the past's search for maximum reliability, and to point out the circularity of most validities.

However, I feel that the paper deals rather inadequately or not at all with a number of important issues.

1 How are the seven (or more) features of language use to be taken account of in communicative language tests?

2 It is important to distinguish between the problem of what language is to be sampled, and how that sample is to be judged.

3 What is the status of the enabling skills? How are they to be adequately measured?

4 The nature of language proficiency is left vague. Is proficiency something a native speaker has and a non-native has to acquire? Does the non-native already possess such proficiency which is merely realised in another language, but which is readily transferable, once one has 'cracked the code'? What is **successful** communication? On what basis are judgements to be made? Who judges, and why? What about the effect of non-linguistic elements like personality, motivation, awareness, and the like on successful outcomes? To what extent is this a purely language problem? To what extent should tests of 'communicative proficiency' be language tests?

5 What is the purpose of the test? Is there not an intimate relation between test purpose, test content and test format which is barely touched upon here? How, precisely, would test content and format be affected by test purpose?

The advantage of testing is that it forces explicitness: the test is an operationalisation of one's theory of language, language use and language learning. Testing is the testing ground for any approach to teaching. If we cannot get the tests our theories seem to require, then we have probably not got our theories right (unless, of course, the theory implies the impossibility of testing). Why has there apparently been such a failure to develop tests consistent with theories of communicative language use?

REPORT OF THE DISCUSSION ON
COMMUNICATIVE LANGUAGE TESTING

J Charles Alderson, University of Lancaster

The most important question to be asked of any test, and communicative language tests are no exception, is what is it measuring? The question that arose in the discussions as to whether what communicative language tests are testing is actually anything different from what has been tested before is a subsidiary and less important issue: although there was a general suspicion that nothing new was being tested in communicative language tests, less agreement was reached on what such tests actually measure.

It is not important that communicative language tests look different from other types of test: what is important is that they measure what one wishes to measure. (There may, however, be good political or administrative reasons why 'communicative language tests' should look different: if they relate to an innovative curriculum which itself appears to be different, a measure of achievement on that curriculum which looked like traditional measures might engender disbelief in either the validity of the measure or the virtues of the new curriculum). However, even though the difference between communicative language tests and other tests may be relatively less important, one reason for comparing the different types of tests is to understand why communicative language testing has developed, and what it is that such tests appear to be measuring.

There would appear to be a variety of dimensions of language in use that existing language tests do not tap. It was generally agreed that existing tests may be unsatisfactory to the extent that they do not cover psycholinguistic abilities, (like enabling skills), or features of language (like unpredictability) which it may be important for students to be exposed to or tested upon. Such features or dimensions derive from two possible sources: either from our theories of language use — that is, our developing theories of the use of language for and in communication generate the dimensions which are to be operationalised in language tests; or they derive from 'real-life': from observations of the world around us at a pre-theoretical, ie descriptive stage.

Attempts to improve existing language tests from the first perspective — that of theory — are attempts to improve the construct validity of the tests; attempts to improve tests from the second perspective, that of mirroring reality in a more adequate fashion, are attempts to improve content validity.

There is a potential conflict between these two validities, in that a theory-derived test may look very different from a real-life derived test. For example, one's theory may include the notion of the transmission of information as being an important component of communication, of language in use. One might then construct a test to measure the quality of such transmission. Upshur's (1971) oral test, for example, is an attempt to do just this, and strives for construct validity. However, it may not look like a real-life situation. When do real people look at a set of four pictures and try to guess which one another person is describing? Tests striving for content validity could constitute job samples, that is, replications of reality, and would therefore inevitably be performance-based. The question is whether tests are mirrors of reality, or **constructed instruments** from a theory of what language is, what language processing and producing are, what language learning is.

In our discussion we were in no doubt that an awareness of the existence of other dimensions has increased in recent years, partly from work in psycholinguistics and sociolinguistics, partly from dissatisfaction with existing tests (either because they do not look right, or because they are thought not to give the results that are required).

However, one evaluates any theory, presumably, by its operationalisation. If operational definitions are not possible, then the theory is poorly stated or inadequate. It is not clear to what extent such operationalisations have been achieved in the construction of communicative language tests, and the view was expressed that possibly the fault lies, not with testers, but with the theories: if they do not permit adequate definitions in test terms, they are not adequate theories. Should one, however, wait for the development of adequate theories of language in use before proceeding with the development of communicative language tests? It was generally felt that this would be inappropriate, especially if it is the case, as seems likely, that a complete theory of communication will not be developed for a very, very long time.

One claimed advantage of communicative tests, or perhaps more accurately performance tests, is that they do not rely on adequate theory for their validity. They do not, for example, make assumptions about the status of competence in a Chomskyan sense, and its relation to performance — its predictive relationship to what people can actually do — because such tests aim to **measure** what people can do. If one is interested in whether students can perform adequately (adequacy being undefined for the moment) at a cocktail party, 'all' one has to do is to put that student into a cocktail party and see how he fares. The obvious problems with this are that it may not always be possible to put the student into a cocktail party (especially if there are several thousand students involved), and the fact that the performance is being assessed may actually change the nature of the performance. One solution to the first problem is to simulate the cocktail party in some way, but that raises problems of authenticity, which relate to the second problem, that of the relationship between the performance and its assessment. Inevitably, any test is in danger of affecting performance if the testee is aware that he is being tested. To that extent, it is impossible for a test to be 'authentic' in the sense of mirroring reality. Of course, tests are themselves authentic situations, and anything that happens in a testing situation, must be authentic in its own terms: the problem comes when one tries to relate that testing situation to some other communicative situation. In a sense, the argument about authenticity is trivial in that it merely states that language use varies from situation to situation. The feeling was expressed that the pursuit of authenticity in our language tests is the pursuit of a chimera: it is simply unobtainable because they are language **tests**.

It was argued that the only interest in authenticity in tests is in the gathering of genuine data (ie data that has occurred) as part of test input. Tests have been developed based upon genuine data, where a real conversation has been recorded, transcribed, and re-recorded using actors reading from the transcription, at least partly in order to ensure good sound quality of the final test. Such practice may be authentic and justified within a testing context, although it probably runs counter to the original reason for gathering data.

Since one cannot, *a priori*, replicate in a test situation what the students will have to face in 'real-life', it was argued that what we should be doing is looking at students' performances on tasks defined according to criterial features, (for example the dimensions mentioned by Morrow like 'unpredictability') and then extrapolate to the outside world. Thus our tasks may not be authentic in the other-world sense, but they have value and validity because we are tapping dimensions, or abilities, which other tests do not tap.

Another, weightier problem than 'authenticity' that was discussed, is that of sampling. If one is interested in students' abilities to perform in cocktail parties, and one somehow measures that ability in one cocktail party, how does one know that in another cocktail party the student will perform similarly? The cocktail party chosen may not have been an adequate sample. This is particularly a problem when we are unable to be as specific about what we want students to be able to do as in this example. If our goals are to measure students' abilities to use language communicatively or to use English in a variety of situations, how are we to decide which tasks to give students in our tests which will adequately represent those goals?

If we are not interested in the students' ability to perform in a situation, but in situations A to Z, then how can we be sure that X is an adequate sample of A — Z. Might not situation B or M be more adequate?

This problem assumes that we are interested in prediction. The question being asked in the debate about sampling is — can we predict from performance on one task to performance on another task or series of tasks? Testing, in other words, is about predicting some criterion behaviour. The assumption of communicative testing, which is an assumption until evidence is produced to justify the notion, is that the only way to predict criterion behaviour is to set up (real) performance tasks. The question is whether one has to put people in to a particular situation in order to find out how they would perform in that situation. The view was expressed that there may be in communicative testing a danger of confusing the 'how' of predicting something, with the 'what' of the prediction. Communicative testing appears to try to bring together the manner and the content (or the test and the criterion) in an arguably unnecessary or indeed impossible manner: the communicative testing argument seems to be that instead of giving somebody a driving test, you put him into a car, and see if he hits the wall. Such assumptions about the need for performance tests need considerable research activity to support them: the discovery of the best predictor (driving test or performance) of the criterion (hitting the wall or not) is an empirical issue.

It may be that the sampling problem is also an empirical issue: in order to find out whether performance on task X is the best predictor of performance on tasks A to Z, one might give subjects a vast array of tasks to perform, and see which is the best predictor. However, predictive validity is not the only type of validity in which we are interested, as we have already seen.

In particular, the traditional proficiency test argument ignores the dimensions of face or content validity. One might argue, from the perspective of predictive validity, that what one is testing does not matter, provided that it predicts the criterion behaviour (performance in a cocktail party). If the best predictor of such behaviour is the size of one's boots, then what one must do is measure students' boots. This argument confuses causality with concomitant variation (students might change the size of boots they are wearing in order to pass the test, but still be unable to perform well in cocktail parties), and generally takes no account of issues like face or content validity.

It was generally agreed that the prior problem in both the sampling debate and the prediction debate, would seem to be that of defining what one wishes to assess, what performance one wishes to sample or predict. First one needs to define what it is that students have to do with language in a specific situation, or series of situations. The danger is that in specifying communicative performance, one might end up describing an impossible variety of situations, which one cannot encompass for testing purposes.

The value of communicative language testing, and the difficulty, is that it represents an attempt to do precisely that: to define the criterion one is trying to sample or predict. Traditionally, proficiency testing at least has been concerned to find the best predictor of a criterion: the argument has run that the best proficiency test is the one which best predicts future behaviour. Thus one might claim that test X is valid because it predicts performance in a cocktail party. The crucial question surely is: what does one know about behaviour in a cocktail party? Gaining that knowledge was felt to be of paramount importance, since it represents the ultimate test. Thus one has to define what it means to perform well in a cocktail party. Once one has described this, one has produced a specification, a set of guidelines, for the construction of the test. Discovering the best predictor of this, or the most adequate sample, is of secondary importance. Thus it may be that the issue of extrapolation is not (yet) of crucial importance: even if we cannot generalise from performance in one situation to performance in a variety of situations, if we can say something about performance in **one** situation, then we have made progress, and if we can say something important about performance in the target situation, so much the better. Ultimately, after all, the student will have to perform, despite the statistical evidence of the relationship between predictor and predicted, or the theorised relationship between competence and performance.

The discussion focussed on what communicative language tests should do or should look like. What is the nature of the tasks which students are given? What makes them different from existing tests, and which features of language use do they take account of? What, for instance, does a communicative test of reading or listening look like? Presumably, a communicative test of reading would be, for example, a set of instructions leading to a behavioural outcome, linguistic or otherwise. The problem with this is that a satisfactory outcome may be reached without 'adequate' linguistic performance. It is possible to devise a vast variety of different tasks: what are the dimensions that must be included to qualify as 'communicative'? A claimed virtue of communicative testing is that it is more explicit about what it is trying to measure than existing tests are: in reading it may result in increased specificity of text type, or type of reading required, although this is not exclusive to communicative testing. This specification may result in an atomistic analysis of behaviours, which, paradoxically, may not be desirable in communicative tests. An interesting result of this consideration is the idea that the so-called dichotomy of communicative testing versus existing tests may be separate from, and unrelated to the (equally arguable) posited dichotomy between discrete-point and integrative tests. In this case, discrete-point communicative tests of reading would be perfectly feasible and justifiable.

The requirement that one analyse situations or target performance in order to establish criteria would appear also to demand an atomistic approach. In order to produce a communicative test, one must, presumably, either sample, or analyse and test. As has been seen, the problem with sampling is that it is difficult to do. However, it would appear that without a prior analysis of performance or tasks, one would have no basis for sampling. Thus, at some level, analysis is essential for communicative testing.

Most communicative testing has been concerned not with reading and listening, but with tests of oral and written production, which have been largely neglected in recent years because of the inherent problem of their reliability. The communicative test of oral production *par excellence* is often said to be the interview (a traditional form of test!). In an interview, the tester can probe and force the students to produce language, based on an inventory of questions and prompts. Typically, he does not work from a list of structures, since, in a communicative test situation, there is no need to think in terms of structural complexity. Interviewers do not deliberately manipulate structures to see if candidates can comprehend or produce them.

One of the dimensions of language in use that was discussed in more detail was that of unpredictability. The argument is that language use is unpredictable, and therefore so should our tests be. To what extent are interviews unpredictable? The interviewer has a set of possible prompts and questions and it would appear that the interview must be highly predictable. However, from the testee's point of view it is considerably less so (he presumably does not know what questions will be asked). What would a test that incorporated the dimensions of unpredictability look like? It would presumably not be a set of question-answer routines (although as was suggested this is less predictable for student than examiner): to what extent are 'unpredictable' tests possible for writing rather than speaking? If, in speaking tests, one requirement is that the responses, and indeed the initiations, should be unpredictable for the examiner, as participant in the interaction, then the question arises of the difficulty of participating in as well as evaluating an interaction that is 'unpredictable'. A common solution to this not unfamiliar problem is to have an interviewer and an observer in the same interview, where the observer is the examiner. This, however, raises the issue of outsider views: is it possible for an outsider to interpret interactions, especially ones which are supposed to be unpredictable? If they are unpredictable what does/can the observer look for? Can criteria be established to allow the assessment of something about whose nature we know little in advance? In any case, different observers will inevitably have different interpretations of events and their quality. This raised the familiar problem in testing: the issue of subjectivity. To what extent in communicative testing is 'objectivity' of assessment attainable, if desirable? It was argued that objectivity is never possible in judgements about language related performance, and that one should simply aim to pool subjective judgements. This does not mean that everybody should agree on one judgement (score), but that judgements are averaged. There is considerable evidence to show that any four judges, who may disagree with each other, will agree **as a group** with any other four judges of a performance. (It was pointed out that it is, however, necessary for markers to agree on their terms of reference, on what their bands, or ranges of scores, are meant to signify: this can be achieved by means of a script or tape library).

Communicative testing has resulted in a focus, not only on the tasks of a test, but also upon the criteria used for assessing performance on those tasks. In particular the British Council has been involved in developing scales and criteria for assessment, which cover areas like appropriacy, amount of communication, content, establishment of communication, and so on. Judges are typically asked, in a non-impression scheme, to rate performances on several dimensions (thought to be relevant to the quality of language in use). One would expect, and indeed one gets, differential performance on different dimensions (such that it is possible to get, say, a three for appropriacy and a five for content), and it is undesirable to add scores on the separate dimensions together in order to arrive at some global assessment, because individual differences will be hidden in such a procedure: what is required is the reporting of some sort of profile. However, the question was raised of the independence of such dimensions, if not in reality, then at least in the ability of judges to rate independently. Cross contamination is quite likely, and only avoidable, if at all, by having different judges rate performances on different dimensions (such that one judge, for example, might rate on appropriacy, whilst another rates on amount of communication). The value of such a procedure would need to be established by empirical research. A problem related to the question of whether the grades given on particular scales actually represent performance on the stated dimension rather than some other dimension, is the question of whether communicative language tests are actually measuring language performance as subsumable under language in use, or whether they are measuring variables that might be said to be extraneous, non-language related. What, for example, is one to conclude about the performance of somebody who, when asked his opinion on a particular topic, does not volunteer anything because he does not have an opinion? Or what is one to make of the shy or introverted student on, say, a discussion test? Particularly in the area of EFL, it is quite likely that there will be cultural differences among testees as to what is acceptable behaviour on performance tasks, which might influence the amount and the quality of the 'behavioural outcome'? What is one to make of that? Must one accept the fact that the measures are not pure measures, on the grounds that 'life is like that', ie people with different cultural backgrounds or personality or cognitive styles will suffer in the real world as well as on our tests?

The point was made that laymen have for a long time expected of language tests that they test language: indeed, such has been the requirement by sponsors of language tests, like the British Council, or the General Medical Council, namely that **only** language should be tested, and 'irrelevant' variables like personality, knowledge of subject matter, opinions and the like, be left out of language tests. To the present-day applied linguist, this looks like a naive oversimplification of the relationship between language and personality, language and thought, language and culture and one might well claim that it is in practice impossible to separate language from these other areas. Yet, since lay people hold such (strong) views on the matter, testers ignore them at their peril.

A further expectation, particularly of sponsors, is that native speakers should do well, even (within the bounds of reliability) perfectly on a language test. Traditionally, proficiency tests were partially validated by reference to native-speaker (perfect) performance. Communicative language tests in particular, though not exclusively, raise the issue of whether native speakers **can** do the task satisfactorily. Which native speakers is one talking about — educated? uneducated? certain professional groups rather than others? Which language is one a native speaker of — English? Medical English? The English used to write inflammatory articles on medical topics in the popular science press in a British context? Are we talking about native speakers who are (the equivalent of) first year under-graduate science students, or eminent and experienced neuro-surgeons? If a native speaker performs poorly on a task, is that because he is the wrong native speaker? Because he lacks the skill or the language? Because he is too clever? One problem that was mentioned with some native speakers on language tests is simply that they are too good: they see ambiguities and difficulties on certain test items that non-native speakers do not see: native speakers can often create plausible contexts for apparently incorrect responses.

Talk, within the field of communicative language testing, of behavioural outcomes, suggests that greatest importance is attached to the product of a communicative interaction. Considerable discussion took place, however, on the question as to whether in communicative language testing, or language testing in general, we need to know how individuals reach their result. Presumably for diagnostic purposes, information on the process is essential, in order to plan some sort of pedagogic treatment or intervention, but is it important to know how results were achieved, for other purposes? Proficiency testing might only be interested in the product, not the process, in which case one might argue that testing enabling skills is inappropriate, because they belong to process. Indeed it was argued that enabling skills may vary from individual to individual, and certain of them may not be used by one person on one occasion to reach a given product, in the performing of a particular task. If one is only interested in the product, then behavioural outcomes are sufficient. If one is interested in knowing whether somebody can cross London, one simply measures whether they get across London, and does not worry about whether they used a map, used Arabic to consult more knowledgeable informants, or followed the written instructions in English that we as test designers had expected them to follow. What is important in this view is whether testees cross London, rather than whether they crossed in some prescribed manner (since in any event in 'real life' it is unlikely that they would follow such prescriptions). It was felt in any case, salutary to make the point that we are ignorant of how people achieve their ends, and that this is impossible to predict, on present knowledge at least, since different individuals will do it in different ways, or even the same individuals will do it differently on different occasions.

Does one need a breakdown of Process in order to construct a valid test task? To validate a test *vis-a-vis* its theory, one would appear to need a breakdown of possible performances on that task. Otherwise, one only has the final outcome for validation purposes. And one does not normally know whether a test is valid simply because people have 'passed' it. However, if one wishes to extrapolate, then one has presumably to talk about underlying skills (ie Process — how people go about doing the task) unless the sampling solution is accepted: 'If you can understand that lecture, then you will be able to understand lectures'. How one understood the lecture, or rather how one arrived at one's understanding of the lecture, is unimportant in this view. Traditional proficiency tests, it was pointed out in the discussion, are not intended to tell one anything at all about students' processes and problems: they 'simply' seek to answer the layman's question: 'Does this man speak English?'

Although the debate about communicative language tests focussed upon the question of what is being measured, it was felt to be impossible to determine what is being measured independently of considerations of how a measure will be validated. In other words, one anticipates the question — 'how do you know?' — as a response to an assertion that a test is a measure of X. How, with communicative language tests, do we know if we have measured what we claim to measure? How can we improve our communicative tests? When designing a new test one must know what one thinks represents an advance and an improvement over existing tests, and there must be some notion of how one can evaluate that, how one can confirm one's suspicion. It was generally agreed as unfortunate that in the world of communicative language testing, there is rather little discussion of how to validate and evaluate such tests, or how they might have been evaluated in the past. One is certainly not absolved from the responsibility of stating one's criteria for validation (not just validity) by the (apparent) absence of other valid tests with which to compare one's own. The argument that one cannot validate a test because there are no other valid tests in existence does not stand up since it appeals only to concurrent validity. One problem with concurrent validation that was touched upon is the problem of interpretation of correlations. If the 'communicative' language test correlates highly with (invalid) discrete point tests, then is this evidence for the invalidity of the test, or for the existence of one general language proficiency. If one observes the (desired) low correlation, does this mean that the test is valid or that it is simply measuring something different, or measuring the same thing rather badly, because of unreliability?

Of course, one way of improving a test is to see what people think is wrong with the existing instrument, for particular purposes, and then see if the new test does the job better. A frequent complaint about proficiency tests is that they fail to identify students who subsequently have problems in their fields of study: they let into institutions students who should have been kept out. Ignoring the fact that test use and test construction are partly separate matters, one might say that such a proficiency test is failing to do its job because it fails to tap relevant skills. The problem is defining those relevant skills. To find out if one's new test is better, one might see how many students passing it actually had problems, (ignoring the difficulties caused by the fact that students who fail are not normally admitted). The problem with this sort of predictive validity is the time factor: one would expect and hope that the correlation between test performance and subsequent problems would decrease as other factors intervene over time, until in the end there would be no correlation. One can see that the extrapolation problem is in fact a validation problem, which relates to the problems of prediction (including the relationship with time factors) common to all language tests, communicative or otherwise. The point about communicative tests is that they make clearer the need to break the circularity of most validation procedures (the circularity consists of correlating with another test or measure) by appealing to outside criteria, because, precisely, of the claim that communicative tests are measures of language in use, 'real' language tests. However, appeal to ideology is not sufficient evidence for accepting the validity of a test. One needs empirical evidence to back up assertions of validity and claims that performance on one task relates to performance on other tasks.

One way of validating tests is to relate them closely to the language teaching that has preceded them. It is at times claimed that communicative language tests are more valid because they relate better to current trends in teaching than do other types of test. There may, however, be good arguments for tests not being in line with teaching (despite the washback effect) because tests can be used as a means of evaluating the teaching; of validating the teaching. If one wishes to know not whether what has been taught has been learnt, but rather whether the right things have been taught, then one needs a test unrelated to the teaching: one needs a proficiency test rather than an achievement test. Thus test purpose should have an effect on test content and form.

Most arguments in favour of communicative language tests are concerned with the validity problem. However, validity is inevitably tied up with reliability: an unreliable test cannot be valid (although an invalid test can be reliable). If one concentrates on validity to the exclusion of reliability, it was pointed out, one needs to ask whether one is **measuring** anything, since measurement is quantification, and with quantification comes the need for reliability. There was general agreement that communicative language tests need to concentrate on improving their reliability. It was argued by some that this means taking the traditional 'pre-scientific' tests, and making them more reliable. One way of improving both validity and reliability of tests is to specify more closely both content and the criteria for assessment. It was felt to be still an open question as to whether communicative language tests have succeeded in doing this, to result in more adequate and successful tests.

One of the problems of communicative language tests is the problem of language in use: it is infinitely variable, being different for different individuals at different points in time. Systematisation (in terms of a theory or a description) seems highly unlikely, and yet desirable for test construction. Language, on the other hand, and more particularly grammar, is relatively systematisable, and therefore usable. In addition, although it may be claimed that communicative language tests are more valid because they relate to students' needs, such validity is relative, since it must depend upon the level of abstraction: what two engineers have in common may be different from what an engineer and a waiter have in common. Inevitably tests are about and for groups of people, not individuals. Levels of abstraction are likely to be higher rather than lower: but it was argued that if one abstracts far enough from a situation or task, one reaches grammar, which is what language learners will need whatever they are going to use the language for, and grammar is the level of language most amenable to systematic description (and therefore it was suggested, incorporation in tests). However, it was generally agreed that linguistic competence can only be a part of communicative competence: and that although one cannot ignore 'grammar' in communicative language tests, one cannot rely exclusively on it. The problem lay in defining precisely what else there is to test.

SECTION 2

SPECIFICATIONS FOR AN ENGLISH LANGUAGE TESTING SERVICE
Brendan J Carroll, The British Council, London

The Testing Problem

1   The present testing system, devised in the earlier half of the 1960's, was in its time a well-thought-out and convenient instrument. Over the years, however, there have been great changes both in the size of the placement problem and in approaches to language test development.

2   The number of applicants for training in Britain has grown out of all recognition over these years. At the same time, there has been an expansion in the range of courses of study required, with increasing emphasis on the applied technologies and on non-university courses and attachments which the earlier test had not been designed to accommodate. This increase in numbers reflects both an emphasis on manpower training schemes under aid programmes and the growing wealth of oil-producing countries in West Africa, South America and the Middle East.

3   Over this period, language teaching and testing methods have shifted their emphasis from atomistic language features, such as uncontextualised phonemic discriminations ('hit — pit') to broader features of linguistic communication. The trend now is, as exemplified in the present report, to postpone consideration of language realisations until the communicative needs of the users have been clearly determined, broadly-speaking a socio-linguistic approach.

4   The trends noted in the previous paragraph have also encouraged the development of programmes in English for Specific Purposes (ESP) so that fewer people are now engaged in devising tests and teaching programmes which aspire to meet equally well the needs of all users, regardless of the purposes for which they will need the language.

5   A recent breakdown of a large group of applicants for courses of study in Britain gives as the five most important categories:

Agriculture (including Fisheries, Timber, Vets.)
Engineering, Medicine (including Dentistry),
Economics (especially re Development) and
Public Administration.

Our problem is not just whether the present test can encompass the needs of these, and many other, diverse study courses, but whether **any** single test can do so. And we have adopted the hypothesis that the solution to our testing problem, and the way to improve the testing service, is through a process of diversification of test instruments to meet the diversity of the test situations.

6 The language test system so developed will have to provide information which will enable us to answer two important questions about any applicant — whether he is already likely to be able to meet the communicative demands of a given course of study or, alternatively, what would be the nature and duration of the course of language tuition he would need in order to reach the required competence level. In designing our testing service, then, we will need to specify the communicative demands of a variety of courses, of different levels, types and disciplines, and to devise workable instruments to measure how far applicants can meet those demands. We must, in doing so, effect a demonstrable improvement on the present system and ensure that the new test itself is capable of continual monitoring and improvement.

Compiling the Specification

1 Purpose of the Specification

Our purpose in compiling the specification is to build up profiles of the communicative needs of a number of students on study programmes in Britain in such a way that we will be able to identify common and specific areas of need upon which an appropriately diversified test design can be based. It is of crucial importance that at this stage our focus is on **the communicative demands the programmes make on the participants.** As we have already said, we will bring to bear on the test design important operational considerations affecting the administration of the test service, but it must be emphasised that such considerations, however pressing, will not make the communicative needs of the participants disappear. We would hardly be likely to achieve our aim of test improvement if we ignored a patently essential communicative need merely because it entailed practical problems.

2 The specification framework

Each specification will provide information about the communicative needs each participant will have in studying his programme and in living in an English-speaking community. The specification parameters are:

0 **Details of the participant;** a minimum amount of potentially relevant information about identity and language

1 **Purpose of Study;** establishing the type of English and the purpose for its use in the programme.

2 **Settings for English;** including both physical and psychosocial settings.

3 **Interactions involved;** identifying those with whom the participant will communicate in English, his position, role relationships and social relationships.

4 **Instrumentality;** the main activity areas — receptive/productive, spoken/written; the channels, face-to-face, print or radio for example.

5 **Dialects of English;** whether British or American English; which regional variety, both for production and reception. Any dialect variations regional, social or temporal.

6 **Proficiency Target Levels;** expressed on a scale from 1 (low) to 7 (high) related to the dimensions of text size, complexity, range and delicacy, and the speed and flexibility of handling it; tolerance conditions expressed on a scale from 1 (low) to 5 (high) related to tolerance of error, style, reference, repetition and hesitation.

7 **Communicative Events and Activities;** the description of what participants have to do, such as 'participating in a seminar' (event) and the parts of those events that assist skill selection later, such as 'putting forward one's point of view' (activity)

8 **Attitudinal Tones;** concerning *how* an activity is enacted; derived from an index of attitudinal tones - sets of antonymous continua such as 'formal-informal'.

9 **Language Skills;** a taxonomy of 54 skill categories, with their component skills, ranging from 'Discriminating sounds in isolated word forms — allophonic variants' to 'Transcoding information in speech/writing to diagrammatic display'.

10 **Micro-Functions;** as exemplified in sub-categories of function; units of meaning between the level of 'activities' and their linguistic realisations, such as the micro-functions of persuasion, advising, invitation.

Note: The specification data in Appendix A are arranged under the section headings, 0 to 10, as above.

3 Areas of specification

English Language Division staff members have prepared specifications of participants in each of the following six areas:

P1 Business Studies (HND)
P2 Agricultural Science (Post-Graduate)
P3 Social Survival (Academic)
P4 Civil Engineering (BSc)
P5 Laboratory Technician (Trainee)
P6 Medicine (FRCS)

Specifications P1, P4 and P6 are for fairly typical English for Academic Purposes (EAP) course participants. P3, Social Survival, relates to the social needs of the average student on an academic programme. P4, Laboratory Technician, is a good example of a sub-University trainee in a non-degree study atmosphere. P2, Agricultural Science, is an unusual but not impossible case where a student requires English almost entirely for the study of reference literature as, being on a two-way programme attachment, he mixes mainly with speakers of his own language or with English staff who speak his language.

It will be seen that a good range of levels and programme types has been included in our sample, although we do not pretend to have covered a representative range of the total population. We hope, however, to elicit from this participant sample, major design factors applicable to test development.

4 Specification data sources

Although it would be desirable to derive our data from comprehensive observational studies of the participants actually engaged on their courses, we decided that less time-consuming methods would be sufficient to assess the basic adequacy of our approach to test specification. **The ultimate validation of our methods would be in the effectiveness of the tests based on their results.** To ensure the best insights possible into this interdisciplinary problem we adopted the following procedures:

a Compilers

The compilers of the profiles were chosen according to their special interests and backgrounds. For example, the Business Studies specification involved two staff members one of whom had published a course in Business English, the other had a degree in Commerce and had lectured in Economics and Accountancy to adults. The Social Survival English profile was compiled by a member of staff who was actually teaching the student concerned on a pre-sessional English course. The Medical profile was prepared by a staff member with considerable experience in teaching a University Medical English course and who had close family connections in Medicine.

b Contacts

All staff concerned made contact with institutions and/or individual lecturers in the disciplines concerned. The Laboratory Technician profile was compiled in discussion with our Technical Training colleagues and in contact with staff and members of a course currently being conducted for Laboratory Technicians. The Civil Engineering profile was prepared by an officer who had earlier done a study of Engineering courses and teaching methods in Britain who was advised by two colleagues in Education and Science Division with appropriate degrees and experience. It is intended that close and continual contacts of this kind will be maintained throughout the process of test development and validation.

c Documents

Continual reference was made to authentic documents in the disciplines such as college handbooks, course syllabuses and standard subject textbooks. We found the widely-used titles circulated under the Low-Priced Text Book Scheme to be of particular value in this respect. To exemplify the exacting demands of the programmes, we include in Appendix D the published requirements for a preparatory course in Civil Engineering.

In general, we believe our data collection methods represent a reasonable compromise between what would be theoretically perfect and what could be done in an acceptable time-scale with resources to hand.

Results of the Specification

We will now examine, in parallel, the results of the six specification studies with the purpose of identifying the essential communicative demands on all the participants. This examination should enable us to identify three levels of communicative demand — those common to all (or most) of the participants, those shared by some groups of participants and not by others, and those specific to an individual participant. In factorial terms we should obtain broad indications of the presence of general, group and specific factors. This information is essential if we are to make firmly-based recommendations about test diversification. Please note that it will not be possible to follow the discussion of results given below without constant reference to the appropriate sections of Appendix A.

0   Details of the Participant

Our purpose in personalising the profile is to focus the collection and interpretation of data on a real, or at least a putative, individual so as to counteract the natural but dangerous tendency to overgeneralise about communicative needs. We are in fact using a simple case-study approach to data collection. Now if we look at Appendix A at Spec. O, the Participant, we see details of our six participants P1 to P6 as regards age, nationality, language and standard of English. The Ps cover a range of countries and native languages, with a certain bias towards Muslim countries, their ages range from twenty to thirty, and their level of English is of Intermediate or Upper-Intermediate standard. It is worth considering at this stage to what extent our sample of course participants is, or needs to be, representative of the total population of candidates for our tests. In earlier approaches to testing, it would be considered necessary to ensure that the sample was representative of the population of candidates as a whole, and the statistics of probability would be used to measure the characteristics of that population; in other words the approach would be 'norm-referenced'.

In our present approach, however, we are starting from the specification of the communicative demands of target courses. Once these demands are defined, it is for us to decide whether a particular candidate has met them on the evidence of his test performance; it is not a matter of primary importance to us how performance characteristics are distributed throughout a population of applicants many of whom, we now know, are likely to be 'non-starters' about whom we are not required to make refined, or delicate, decisions. Our approach, then, is basically 'criterion-referenced' and our performance standards will derive from ongoing courses and their students. In our recommendations, we will put forward proposals which take into account the existence of these 'non-starters'.

1   Purpose of Study (Appendix A, Spec. 1)

We see from the information given that two of the participants are engaged in post-graduate study, two in undergraduate study and one in sub-university training. One of the specifications, P3, does not have a training focus. There is a fair range of disciplinary studies — Medicine, Agriculture, Business and Applied Technology. We are not, of course, centrally concerned with the disciplines as such but with the communicative demands their programmes make on the students, and their consequential communicative needs. It will be a matter of great interest to discover how far disciplinary domains coincide with or diverge from communicative domains.

2 Settings for English (Appendix A, Spec. 2)

It is immediately obvious that although there is a variety of programmes there is considerable uniformity in their physical settings. In all instances, we find the Lecture room, Seminar room and the Library or Study centre. There is a general need for practical or field work — on site, in industry or in the casualty ward. For the more technologically-oriented participants there is a need for work in the laboratory, workshop or operating theatre.

The Agricultural Science student, whom we have already discussed as the odd-man-out regarding study needs, will use his own language extensively except for reference reading and use English in a restricted range of settings. And all students, however retiring their nature, will be living in English-speaking communities with Social Survival requirements as outlined in the P3 profile.

The temporal settings indicate that, again with the exception of P2, English will be used many hours a day in term time and even extensively in vacations. It is salutary to realise how heavy this avalanche of language demands is for students who so often have had little practical experience of English as a communicative tool, who are confronted with new approaches to their subject and who come from a cultural background very different from, and even inimical to, their new environment.

3 Interactions (Appendix A, Spec. 3)

The importance of interactions for our participants is shown in the variety of relationships recorded in the specifications. The most commonly-mentioned interactions, both within the programme and outside it, are:

Learner-instructor (and, for the Medical student, vice versa)
Professional-professional (in mixing with course staff and members)
Senior-junior (possibly re age, but more probably in the academic context)
Outsider-insider (as a foreigner, and as a newcomer to his groups)
Insider-insider (within national, student or academic groups)
Adult-adult (none of the P's has a major concern with children)
Man/woman-man/woman (in permutations)
Equal-equal (both socially and academically)

The largest range of interactions occurs in P6, the Medical participant. As a senior medical person, this participant is by turn lecturer, adviser, therapist and leader as well as having a student role. The Laboratory Technician, P5, will also occupy a non-student role and, as an older and more experienced person, will be occupying non-student positions in preparation for his future duties as trainer and supervisor. It is thus important to realise that some of the trainees and scholars do not come to Britain in a humble role of tutelage but are likely to be put in positions of professional and personal leadership for which they must be linguistically fitted if they are not to suffer grave loss of face.

4 Instrumentality (See Appendix 1, Spec. 4)

We can see that both receptive and productive skills and spoken written media are required. We will see from the next section that the relative importance of the four communicative media (listening, speaking, reading and writing) will vary considerably from profile to profile.

The main channels are the conventional ones of face-to-face and print. With the increase in use of modern mechanical devices, we must also consider the use of sound and video tapes, audio and video cassettes, radio, television, the telephone and public address systems. This variety of channels contrasts with the very restricted range commonly used in language testing and suggests the possibility of widening the range of test presentations.

5 Dialect (Appendix 1, Spec. 5)

The common need is for contemporary English (Historical or Literary studies might have provided exceptions). The participants will need to understand varieties of standard British English and local varieties of English to be heard in their area of residence. They will be expected to produce intelligible and acceptable standard English varieties of their home region (eg West African), probably with a local accent (eg Northern Nigerian). The main basic requirement will be a certain flexibility in understanding a range of English accents and the ability to produce a variety of English intelligible to the other members and the staff of their own course.

6 Target Level (Appendix 1, Spec. 6)

In specifying the target level we need to know for the first dimension (size) the size of the text the participant will have to handle, for the second dimension (complexity), the complexity of the text, and so on for each of the six variables listed in Spec. 6. Each of these dimensions is assessed on a 7-point scale from very low (1) to very high (7) and derived from the purpose of study and the type of interaction for the participant.

The participants' situation may also allow various degrees of tolerance of error, stylistic failure, use of reference sources, repetition or re-reading and hesitation or lack of fluency. This tolerance is assessed on a 5-point scale from low (1) to high (5) tolerance. It must be admitted that the assessments given by the compilers were subjective ones and we have not yet been able to calculate the reliability of the rating system. We must therefore not read too refined an interpretation into our analysis.

a   Verbal Medium

For purposes of comparability we have used percentages (rather than a 1 to 7 scale) to express the averages of the dimension ratings in Spec. 6. For each participant we give the average percentage rating for each of the four verbal media: Listening, Reading, Speaking and Writing, as well as the averages for each row and column, in Table 1 below.

Table 1:   Average Ratings % for Target Level Dimensions

Participant	Listening	Reading	Speaking	Writing	Average
P1 Business Studies	81	76	60	67	71
P2 Agric. Science	26	69	17	36	37
P3 Social Survival	74	60	50	14	50
P4 Engineering	81	79	52	57	67
P5 Lab. Technician	79	67	52	36	59
P6 Medicine	83	83	64	60	73
Overall averages	71	72	49	45	59

Even if we accept that the ratings in the table look more precise than they actually are, we can see very different types of profile for the various participants. The overall pattern of demand is for a high level for the receptive media (71 and 72) and a much lower level for productive media (49 and 45) indicating the fairly obvious fact that the participants play a responding rather than an initiatory role in the learning situation. The three EAP examples, P1, P4 and P6 have rather similar need profiles, with P6 (Medicine) having probably the most demanding one (average 73). Of the remaining three profiles, P2 (Agricultural Science) is the most remark-- able, with a high demand only in reading and an overall average demand of only 37.

We will show, in Table 2 below, a graphic representation of the two extreme profiles P6 and P2 to illustrate perhaps the most significant conclusion to be obtained from the present report, namely that the pattern of demands of the various programmes can be very different both overall and for the individual verbal media. Admittedly we have, for illustrative purposes, chosen the two extreme cases but the same considerations, in less extreme form, will apply to the other profiles.

Table 2: Comparison of Medical (P6) and Agricultural (P2) profiles

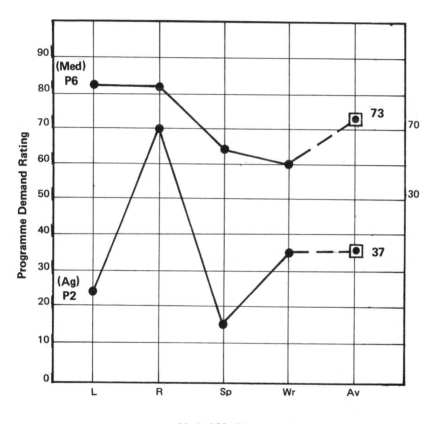

Verbal Medium

The first point to note is that the profiles are not level, but subject to considerable rise and fall across the scale, indicating that the average demand rating should not be used unqualified as an estimate of the difficulty of a programme. In the above case, a student with a level profile of 50 (assuming that we have devised comparable profile calibrations for both programme demands and student competence)would be above the average rating of 37 for P2, but would be below standard on his reading rating. A student with a level profile of 70 would be above the level of all demands for P2 but still fall short in listening and reading modes for P6. The important point we wish to make, and to which we will return later in the report, is **that in making placement decisions we must match the profile of programme demands with the profile of candidate performance.** This conclusion is extremely significant in that we can now achieve our object of improving our test system not only by improving the precision and relevance of the tests themselves (the centre of our negotiations so far) but also by clarifying and making more precise the communicative demands of the various programmes.

b   Tolerance Conditions

We will not go into such detail in our analysis of the ratings for tolerance conditions because indications are in the same direction as those reached in the previous section.

The different programmes have their own respective patterns of tolerance level and the tolerance ratings are negatively correlated with the level of demand; in other words high demand on performance goes with low tolerance, and vice versa.

One conclusion from the tolerance conditions analysis is that the least tolerance is, broadly speaking, extended to language errors and the most to deficiencies in style, recourse to reference sources and to repetition. We can thus conclude that correctness of language usage — lexis, grammar, spelling, punctuation, etc — is by no means an unimportant component of communicative competence in study programmes, although, as we already observed, this correctness should be judged in a communicative context; the higher level skills of scanning, evaluation and logical deduction, for example, cannot be exercised in a linguistic vacuum. This is a consider-- ation that enthusiasts for the communicative approach have been in danger of forgetting.

Apart from the ratings of tolerance we have been considering, there is one important polarity which placement agencies have been very familiar with and which derives from the autonomy of British educational institutions and their departments. This is that it is for the Head of a Department to decide whether or not an applicant is to be accepted on a programme. At one extreme we may have a post-graduate course in Medicine which is already over-subscribed and whose Head is naturally concerned with retaining very high standards of competence if only because the students' decisions will often be a matter of life and death. At the other extreme, we may have the Head of a Science Department in a College of Further Education whose students come almost wholly from overseas and whose staff would be courting redundancy if they rejected applicants because they had language problems.

It is clear that for the former type of department, our testing and tuition must be such as to guarantee that the students have reached the required level of communicative competence before they embark on their course of study. In the latter type, whilst it will still be necessary to establish programme demands and student competence levels, there will be much more scope for concurrent language tuition and, no doubt, for the provision of special bridging courses in which attention can be given both to the improvement of language and to subject skills.

These considerations reinforce our earlier conclusion about the need to match course demands and student competence levels. A clear, intelligible system for presenting the two kinds of information should therefore be available so that Heads of Departments will have to hand a convenient instrument for making placement decisions.

7 Events and Activities (Appendix A, Spec. 7)

Events are what the participants have to do by virtue of the training programme they have undertaken. A typical event would be 'Attending a lecture in the main subject area', and this event could be broken down into component activities such as:

'listening for overall comprehension'
'making notes on main points of lecture',
and 'asking questions for clarification'.

From the topics treated in the events are derived the significant lexical items and lexical sets to be used on academic programmes. It should be noted, however, that language realisations are not derived directly from these activities out via skills and socio-semantic units described later.

The events and activities recorded in Spec. 7 reinforce the information about settings already discussed. The main study focuses are lectures, seminars/tutorials, reference study, report writing, laboratory work, and practical work in industry, on field projects and in hospitals. The extent to which Social Survival English should play a part in the assessment process has been the subject of some controversy. On the one hand, trainees in Britain will need some mastery of the kind of English used in social interactions; on the other hand, as the language formulae are heavily culture-bound, it may be unreasonable to expect candidates to be familiar with them in the way that they could be expected to be with the type of discourse used in their own subject areas. We are on the point of completing a new profile, P7, based on 'English for International Use', which may provide a compromise in this area of Social English.

8 Attitudinal Tone Index (Appendix A, Spec. 8)

The communication units derived from the specified activities (and referred to again in our next section on micro-functions) are marked for attitudinal tone. It is the expression and recognition of attitudes which often pose to non-native speakers their greatest problem, and is usually the area of language training which is the most neglected. In our specification, no less than forty-three attitudinal tone continua are recorded. We list below thirteen of these tones which we judge to be most important partly in view of their frequency of occurrence:

Pleasant-unpleasant
Cautious-incautious (p)
Caring-indifferent
Formal-informal(p)
Grateful-ungrateful(p)
Honest-dishonest(p)
Disinterested-biased

Respectful-disrespectful
Approving-disapproving(p)
Inducive-dissuasive(p)
Certain-uncertain(p)
Intelligent-unintelligent
Assenting-dissenting(p)

The participants are expected to recognise manifestations of all these tones and to be able to produce those marked (p).

9 Language Skills (Appendix A, Spec. 9)

The activities listed in Spec. 7 may also be realised in terms of language skills contained in the fifty-four skill categories of our model and listed as a taxonomy in Appendix A. For practical purposes of test development, this area of specification is of the greatest importance. We have recorded for each skill any profile which refers at least once to that skill.

On the assumption that any skill recorded for 4, 5 or all of the profiles is likely, because of the heterogeneity of our participants, to be of a general, or non-disciplinary, nature and the skill category to be of broad significance, we mark such skills with an asterisk below. We also list other skills categories for which there are skills with 3 occurrences as well as a small number whose absence would give inconsistency to our list.

List of Essential Language Skill Categories

Skill Category	Abbreviated Title
4	Articulating sounds in connected speech.
7/8	Recognising and manipulating stress variations in connected speech.
9/10	Recognising and manipulating stress for information, emphasis and contrast.
11/12	Understanding and producing neutral intonation patterns.
13/14	Interpreting and expressing attitudinal meaning through intonation.
15	Interpreting attitudinal meaning through pitch, pause and tempo.
17/18*	Recognising and manipulating the script.
20/21*	Understanding and expressing explicit information.
24/25*	Understanding and expressing conceptional meaning.
26/27*	Understanding and expressing communicative value.
19	Deducing meaning of unfamiliar lexical items.
22*	Understanding information not explicitly stated.
28/29*	Understanding relations within the sentence.
30/31	Understanding and expressing relations through lexical cohesion devices.
32/33*	Understanding and expressing relations through grammatical cohesion devices.
35*	Recognising indicators in discourse.
37/38	Identifying and indicating main point of discourse.
39*	Distinguishing main idea from supporting details.
40/41*	Extracting salient points of text.
43*	Reduction of text.
44*	Basic techniques of text layout and presentation.
45	Skimming a text.
46	Scanning a text.
47/48*	Initiating and maintaining a discourse.
51/52*	Transcoding.information (diagram/language)

If a test were devised using the skill categories marked with an asterisk, it would cover the main language skill needs of all types of participant. In framing the test items we would refer to the Target Level indices and the topic areas provided by the specifications. The skills covered in the categories between 4 and 15, which we might call the lower-level skills, tend to be related to profiles P3, P5 and P6, indeed 84% of occurrences in these categories occur in respect of those three profiles indicating the existence of an EOP (English for Occupational Purposes) group factor. Further analysis of the factor pattern suggested by the Language Skill analysis is of the highest importance and is to be found in Section 3 below.

10 Micro-Functions (Appendix A, Spec. 10)

The use of the term 'function' is currently a matter of extended debate, and for a detailed discussion of its use in the present document one must refer to J Munby's thesis. For present purposes, however, we will define the micro-function as representing an inter-level between events (with their component activities) and their linguistic realisation. When we have specified an event and its component activities, we are not yet in a position to generate language realisations. This process can be carried out via the selected language skills categorised in Spec. 9 with particular reference to skill categories 26 and 27 related to the communicative value (or function) of an utterance; or it may be done by selecting the appropriate micro-functions from Spec. 10 (affirmation, certainty, negation, etc) and marking them for attitudinal tone from the index given in Spec. 8.

We suggest that none of the micro-functions in the 7 categories given in Spec. 10 are to be ignored. It may be best in practice to base test items on a good coverage of the important skill taxonomy items suggested in Spec. 9 and to support them with relevant socio-semantic units derived from the list of Micro-functions marked with appropriate items from the index of Attitudinal Tones, the latter half of the process being particularly relevant to the less academic communicative activities.

This suggested procedure can be checked for its value during the test development phase.

Implications for Test Design

1 The various conclusions arising from the analysis of our sample specifications have now to be drawn together so that specific proposals for test design and development can be made. It will be prudent first to reiterate our reservations about the data:

a The six participant types we have selected do not purport to be a representative sample of the levels and disciplines of the total testee population.

b The field work so far done depends too much on the subjective judgements of the compilers and too little on close, extended observation of learning situations.

c The reliability of the target level ratings cannot be vouched for and they should only be used to support broad conclusions.

In spite of these reservations, however, we should not forget that the present approach to test design via the detailed specification of communicative needs is a breakthrough, and a considerable advance on the traditional approach to test design based either on purely linguistic categories (vocabulary, structure), on the convenience of particular test types (cloze, multiple-choice,) discrimination of phonemes or on hybrids of language categories and communicative tasks (reading comprehension, interviews) supported by norm-referenced statistics of probability. It is not that any of the above features are irrelevant, it is just that they do not operate in a coherent communicative framework.

2 Range of Communicative Demands

On studying the various profiles, one is struck by the very wide range of communicative demands the programmes make on the participants. This wide range — of skills, topics, channels, verbal media, interactions and functional categories — exists even in apparently the most simple programmes. We are bound to conclude that conventional tests are covering too narrow a range of communicative and language requirements; this fact may explain the disappointing results which validation studies of language testing so often produce.

3 Common and specific factors

We have used the taxonomy of Language Skills to study the pattern of relationships existing between the various disciplines. Using the data of Appendix A, Spec. 9, we have recorded for each skill category all co-occurrences of all Ps; in pairs, in threes, in fours, in fives, and those skills recorded in all six P's or for only one P. The data give us indices of the amount of communicative overlap between the various disciplinary programmes which we assume to indicate similarities of demand between them. We illustrate our findings in Table 3 in the shape of a network, the number of lines indicating the strength of the relationship between any two programmes; to keep the diagram intelligible we have omitted small or negligible relationships.

The main network feature is a clearly-defined star-pattern with Medicine (P6) strongly related to Business Studies (P1) and to Social Survival (P3), and fairly strongly to Laboratory Technician (P5) and Engineering (P4).

The second main network feature is the isolated position of Agricultural Science (P2).

Table 3: Language Skill Network

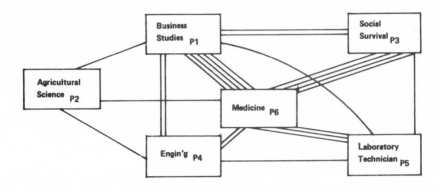

The third network feature is the position of Business Studies (P1) as itself the centre of a subsidiary cluster related to all the other Ps and as a satellite of P6.

The conclusion we draw from these relationships is a perfectly clear one, **that Language Skill requirement patterns cut right across disciplinary boundaries;** indeed, in this study, we find the smallest communicative relationships between disciplines which seem to have the most in common, eg Engineering and Technician, both in the applied technology field.

We have not carried out such detailed work on other specification areas but a rapid check on overlap of attitudinal tones suggests a similar sort of conclusion about communicative features and disciplinary boundaries.

This finding has important implications for test design, but still leaves us with a major unsolved problem. Even if the Medical and Business Studies programmes we have considered are highly correlated communicatively, it still remains that the spoken and written discourse of the two disciplines are very different indeed; their linguistic and diagrammatic realisations have very different appearances. Can we then test different disciplines with identical test material, selected to test their common communicative requirements? Or will we, in doing so, use over-generalised language/diagram realisations which may favour candidates in one particular discipline or, worse still, be equally irrelevant to all the disciplines? We are not yet in a position to answer these questions, so we propose to continue in a pragmatic fashion by preparing tests in different disciplinary areas and by paying particular attention in test data analysis to assessing any benefits, in improved test effectiveness, which can be related to diversification on a disciplinary basis.

Pending a full statistical analysis of future test results, we put forward a tentative assessment of the factor pattern underlying our network diagram in Table 3:

Factor I: 'general' factor, accounting for a sizeable proportion (perhaps half) of the variance, representing the common communicative requirements and characteristics (intelligence, motivation, academic aptitude) of all participants.

Factor II: an 'Academic Study' factor reflecting the ability to use the communication/language skills necessary for handling academic discourse of a relatively neutral attitudinal nature.

Factor III: a 'Personal Relationships' factor representing non-study relationships with contacts in field or clinical work.

Factors IV + : Specific or small-group factors representing the special additional requirements of odd-man-out programmes.

4 Testing versus Matching;

It will be remembered that earlier (in Section 6. a) we reached a conclusion of the greatest operational significance, that considerable improvement in placement efficiency could be achieved not only by improving the tests themselves but also by matching the competencies of the candidates with the communicative demands of the programmes, on a profile basis. This close integration cannot be achieved if the testing service is seen as an autonomous, separately - conducted operation in the manner of a periodically-set Proficiency examination. Nor will test efficiency be improved if tests are based mainly on formal language considerations divorced from programme communicative requirements. The closer the involvement of the receiving institutions and placement agencies in the assessment process, the more likely they will be to conduct an efficient placement service.

5 A framework for measurement

We have already established the value of comparing, or matching, candidate performance with programme demands. What we now need is a common scale upon which we can plot in a comparable fashion, the profiles which express significant dimensions of the two types of assessment. This framework should be intelligible to the non-specialist staff who have to make day-to-day decisions about the placement of thousands of applicants. We give in Table 4 an illustration of such a framework.

Let us suppose we are rating programme demands, and testing student performance, on six dimensions — listening, reading, speaking, writing, integrated skills and the average of all these scores. We show, in the framework, profiles for the programme (P) and for two students (A) and (B). To allow for rating and scoring unreliability we assume a margin of error of 4 points which can be visualised as a grey area 4 points above or below P. Our placement officer is asked to make the classic decisions for Students A and B — whether they are acceptable as they stand or, alternatively, what type of language tuition they may require before acceptance. This task, which in normal cases he should find a good deal easier than filling in his Income Tax return, is done by reference to the respective profiles.

Table 4: Matching programme demands and student proficiency

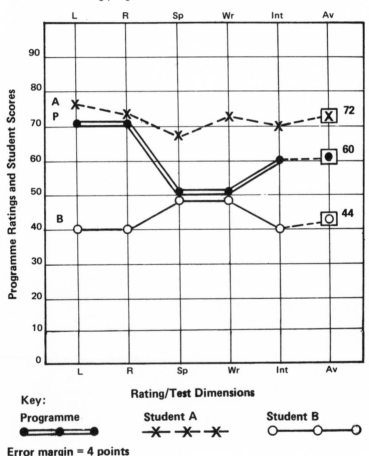

Key:

Rating/Test Dimensions

Programme
●━━●━━●

Student A
✕ -✕- ✕

Student B
○━━○━━○

Error margin = 4 points

Student A, even allowing for any errors of measurement, is significantly above the profile, P, in all dimensions and he can be recommended for acceptance (in respect of his communicative competence) without qualification. The chances of his having language problems on his course of study are very small indeed.

Student B, however, is significantly below the Programme Rating in 3 areas, listening, reading and integrated skills; and just below, although not significantly so, in speaking and writing. He will therefore require language tuition before his course begins. A decision then has to be made about the nature and duration of his tuition. As his main deficiencies are in the receptive media and in integrated skills, some emphasis on those areas will be recommended. The extent of his deficiency can be counted in terms of bands, ie 3 bands each for L and R and 2 bands for Int, or 8 bands in all. Let us assume an average tuitional requirement of 25 hours per band, then we will recommend 200 hours of language tuition. The bases for such estimates can be made more precise in the light of experience.

Such a matching system would not only improve our placement process but could also effect considerable economies in pre-course tuition — an extremely expensive activity — because we would now have much more precise guidance about the nature and duration of the tuition than we could have obtained by comparing a student's average score with a vague estimate of course requirements, a hit-or-miss procedure which runs the risk of providing over-tuition for certain students and under-tuition for others.

6 Syllabus Implications

In preparing the test content specifications for our participants, we have at the same time been specifying essential parts of the syllabus content specification for teaching purposes because we cannot specify test requirements in a curricular vacuum. This double result is, however, a fortunate one for our Testing Service as we now have ready to hand a tuitional blueprint to supplement the placement system. The detailed work on specification, then, has not been nugatory but has added a significant dimension to the operational resources of the testing/tuition service overall.

7 Test Format

In our preparatory work, we have had no difficulty in devising test types to measure the varied communicative features revealed in the specifications, indeed the range of activities brought up has been a valuable stimulus to test development. It is not the devising of test formats which has been the problem, but the making of an operational framework in which to deploy them. We will in our proposals give an outline of a test format which we consider relevant, but we emphasise that the central point of this report is the specification of communicative needs and demands and that discussion of test formats should not by-pass the crucial area of specification.

Operational Requirements

In this section, we will focus our attention on the operational requirements of overseas representations and training/scholarships departments but we must remember that they are working basically on behalf of the British institutions of all kinds, Universities, Colleges and Research Institutes, who actually receive the students. Here are the main operational requirements:

1   Tests must be readily available at all times of the year. Several representatives have said that to arrange fixed dates for test applications (say three or four times a year) would introduce intolerable delays in the manpower training cycle.

2   Results of the tests must be available within days or even hours of their administration to candidates. One senior representative for example has said that if he has to wait for more than a week for results he will not be able to use the Test Service.

3   Clear guidance must be available to assist staff in interpreting test results for placement and/or tuition purposes.

4   In certain countries there are large numbers of candidates (estimates vary between 50% and 80%) who have no reasonable chance of achieving any kind of satisfactory pass performance. A rapid screening device for identifying such candidates is urgently needed.

5   Most representatives are keen to see an improvement in the efficiency of the testing service but wish to achieve this with the minimum of increase to their administrative load.

6   The cost of testing is a sensitive issue. Considerable opposition to a proposed fee of £10 plus local costs has been demonstrated. Different regions of the world vary considerably in their reactions to price increases.

7   Security of tests is important, particularly as versions of the present test are known to have been compromised. This does not mean that every test has to be a completely new one, but that alternative versions should be available, and old versions should be replaced, at a rather faster rate than they are at present.

8   In small representations or where professional ELT resources are not available, the application, marking and interpretation of tests may require external assistance on a regional or central basis.

9   Areas with large Direct English Teaching operations have considerable resources available for testing.

10   There will always be unusual or specially urgent demands for testing not catered for within any broadly applicable test framework. Exceptions must be allowed for.

Overall, the variety of requirements of 70 or 80 representations and up to 120 countries demands a flexible (even untidy) approach to language assessment if a large and complex manpower programme is to maintain its operational momentum.

Recommendations for a Language Testing Service

1   We now put forward for consideration a number of recommendations concerning the design and development of the testing service. In framing the recommendations, we have aimed to give balanced consideration to the findings of our specification analyses, to the practical constraints upon those who have to operate the service and to commonsense considerations about what is feasible in present circumstances.

Recommendation 1 — Test Phases

That a two-level testing pattern be adopted with the following phases:

Phase A   A broad-span, easily-administered screening test in listening and reading skills, covering in a non-disciplinary manner the receptive Language Skill categories 20, 24 and 26, (information handling, conceptual meaning and communicative value) and Skills 30, 32, 37, 39 and 40.

Phase B   A modular test pattern covering the communication skills appropriate to about 6 major disciplinary areas with sizeable numbers of candidates. These disciplinary tests should be supplemented by an Academic Communication Skills test designed for applicants who are not certain about their course of study, who are not adequately catered for in the existing disciplinary modules or are undertaking inter-disciplinary studies.

87

Recommendation 2 — Marking

That Phase A be marked in an objective manner and capable of being applied, marked and interpreted locally by non-specialist staff. That Phase B should be marked in as objective a manner as possible but may contain features requiring trained assistance for application and assessment.

Recommendation 3 — Interpretation

That the principle of matching students to course demands be accepted and a profile framework be devised to facilitate interpretation of test results.

Recommendation 4 — Development

That a test development team be specially trained in the use of specification techniques and the devising of tests derived from them and to prepare two parallel versions of a Phase A test and one version of a test for each of the Phase B areas.

2 A Sample Testing Pattern

Before a firm test pattern can be devised, decisions on the recommendations above will have to be made and the number and content of modular areas will have to be ascertained. We put forward a 'shadow' test pattern, subject to modification, as follows:

Phase A.   Reading Test (approx 50 minutes)

1 **Test of conceptual meaning skills** in Skill Category 24 and relations within sentence, Skill 28. (50 items, m/choice, discrete)

2 **Test of communicative value,** Skill 26, and Lexical and Grammatical cohesion devices, Skills 30 and 32. (50 items, modified m/choice cloze type)

3 **Understanding of information,** Skill 20, with component of Attitudinal Tone input (Spec. 8) and Communicative Value, Skill 26 (and Spec 10) (30 m/choice items based on texts)

Listening Test (approx 30 minutes)

1 **Recognition of shapes,** diagrams and pictures from taped descriptions, testing conceptual meaning, Skill 24. (30 multiple-choice items)

2 **Recognition of short sentences** from taped descriptions testing conceptual meaning, Skill 24 and function, communicative value, Skill 26. (30 multiple-choice items)

3 **Comprehension of a lecturette** of about 3 minutes, test of recognition of facts, Skill 20 and identifying main point as in Skills 37, 39 and 40 (20 multiple-choice items)

Phase B   Modular Tests   (approx 100 minutes)

[Possible areas:— Agriculture, Medicine, Science, Technology, Administration, Education; plus General Academic test based on English for academic and international use]

1 **Reading Study Skills test;** of Skills numbered between 22 and 52, especially the starred skills, based on information booklet on topic area. (40 multiple-choice items with same accepted alternatives for all modules to facilitate marking)

2 **Writing Skills test;** problem-solving, descriptive and reference skill writing based on information booklet. (Subjective rating according to scale and with photo'ed samples of examples at different levels)

3 **Structured Interview;** in cases where there is high demand and low tolerance for speech skills. (Subjective rating on detailed scale and based on information booklet. Cassette samples of different levels available)

Time Limits. As tolerance for time/fluency is fairly high, it is recommended that time limits should be fairly generous and allow the normal student to complete most of the items. Overseas, a good deal of testing will be confined to Phase A (Reading Test) and perhaps A (Listening Test) and a comparatively small number may do all parts. In UK, the interest will probably shift to Phase B especially for University entrance purposes.

APPENDIX A

Specification of Communicative Needs

	The Participant	P1. Business	P2. Agriculture
Spec. 0	Age Nationality Language English Std	20's Nigerian Hausa Intermediate	20's Venezuelan Spanish Elementary
Spec. 1	Purpose of study		
	Course	HND Business Studies Polytechnic	Post Graduate Agricultural Studies University (English for Reference)
	Study Areas	Business Studies: Economics, Law, Business Accounts, Statistics Marketing, Purchasing	Agriculture: Cattle breeding, Animal husbandry, Physiology
	General Area	Social Sciences	Biological Sciences
Spec. 2	Setting for English		
	Physical	Lecture room Tutorial room Library Factories Business offices	Lecture rooms Laboratories Library Bookshop
	Temporal	Full-time in term, plus vacations, Av: 10 hours per day	In English classes In term-time 10 hours per week Less in vacation
Spec. 3	Interactions	*Learner-instructor *Outsider-insider Non-professional- professional *Non-native-native *Insider-insider *Adult-adult	Learner-instructor Non-native-native Insider-insider Adult-adult *Professional- professional

Note: Interactions recorded three or more times are marked with an asterisk

90

P3. Social	P4. Engineering	P5. Technician	P6. Medicine
20's Turkish Turkish Upper intermed.	20's Sudanese Arabic Intermediate	30 Ethiopian Amharic Intermediate	26 Saudi Arabic Upper Intermed.
Academic Studies at University - (Social purpose)	BSc in Civil Engineering University	Experience as Medical Lab. Technician Hospital/College	Post Graduate studies in Medicine for FRCS. Teaching Hospital
not specified; social survival for specific study area	Engineering: all branches (gen) Maths, Electrical Science, Thermo- fluids, Mechanics, Surveying, Project Finance & appraisal	Medic Lab Techniques: Physical Sciences Biological Sciences Para-medical Workshop practice	Medical Studies: Anatomy, Surgery, General Medicine, Consultancy & Casualty work
	Engineering Science	Mixed Technology	Medicine
On campus, Canteens, cafes offices, Houses, Places of Enter- tainment Sports places	Lecture halls Workshops Laboratories Library Tutorial rooms Field sites	College Hospital Teaching areas Library Workshop	Hospital surgery wards Operating theatre Lecture rooms Seminar rooms Library Common Room
Daily use 10-12 hours per day throughout year	Daily, all day Up to 10 hours p day	Weekdays 6 hours, less at weekends, During training course	5 days per week 9 hours + per day Regularly whilst in UK

Learner-instructor
Outsider-insider
Beneficiary-
  benefactor
Non-native-native
Insider-insider
Adult-adult
Professional-
 	
  professional
*Junior-senior(+vv)
Advisee-adviser
*Man/woman-
  man/woman
*Equal-equal
Friend-friend
Guest-host
	Learner-instructor
	Outsider-insider
	Non-native-native
	Adult-adult
	Professional-
	  professional
	Junior senior
	Man/woman-man/
	  woman
	Student-student
		Learner-instructor
		Non-native-native
		Insider-insider
		Adult-adult
		Professional-
		  professional
		Equal-equal
		Man/woman-man/
		  woman
		Customer-server
		Member of pub-official
		Guest-host
			Learner-instructor
			    (+vv)
			Therapist-patient
			Adviser-advisee
			    (+vv)
			Consultant-client
			Leader-follower
			Adult-adult
			Professional-
			  professional
			Professional-
			  non-professional
			Senior-junior (+vv)
			Equal-equal

	Instrumentality	P1. Business	P2. Agriculture
Spec. 4	<u>Medium</u>	Listening Speaking Reading Writing	as P1
	<u>Mode</u>	Monologue Dialogue	as P1
		(spoken and written to be heard or read; sometimes to be spoken as if not written)	
	<u>Channel</u>	Face-to-face Print Tape Film	Face-to-face Print
Spec. 5	<u>Dialect</u>	All sections: Understand British Standard English dialect. Produce acceptable regional version of Standard English accent.	

Spec. 6 <u>Target Level</u>   (in the 4 media for each section)

<u>Dimensions:</u>		L	Sp	R	Wr	L	Sp	R	Wr
(max=7)	Size	6	3	7	3	2	1	7	3
	Complexity	7	4	6	5	2	1	6	3
	Range	5	4	5	5	2	1	4	2
	Delicacy	5	5	6	6	1	1	5	3
	Speed	6	4	5	6	3	2	5	3
	Flexibility	5	5	3	3	1	1	2	1
<u>Tolerance</u> Conditions		L	Sp	R	Wr	L	Sp	R	Wr
(max=5)	Error	3	4	3	3	4	5	1	2
	Style	4	4	5	4	5	5	4	4
	Reference	3	4	2	2	5	5	3	3
	Repetition	3	4	2	3	5	5	5	3
	Hesitation	3	4	4	3	4	5	3	3

P3. Social   P4. Engineering   P5. Technician   P6. Medicine

P3. Social	P4. Engineering	P5. Technician	P6. Medicine
as P1	as P1	as P1	as P1
as P1	as P1	as P1	as P1
Face-to-face Telephone Print Public address Radio TV Disc Tape recorder Film	Face-to-face Print Film Pictorial Mathematical	Face-to-face Telephone Radio Print Tape recorder	Face-to-face Telephone Print

Dialect

All sections: Understand British Standard English dialect. Produce acceptable regional version of Standard English accent.

L	Sp	R	Wr	L	Sp	R	Wr	L	Sp	R	Wr	L	Sp	R	Wr
4	3	4	1	6	3	7	3	6	4	5	3	6	5	6	4
4	3	4	1	6	5	6	5	6	3	5	3	6	4	6	4
7	3	5	1	5	4	6	4	6	5	6	3	6	4	6	4
4	4	4	1	6	4	6	5	6	5	6	3	6	5	6	5
6	4	4	1	6	3	4	4	6	3	5	2	5	4	5	4
6	4	4	1	5	3	4	3	3	2	1	1	6	5	6	4

L	Sp	R	Wr	L	Sp	R	Wr	L	Sp	R	Wr	L	Sp	R	Wr
3	4	3	5	1	3	3	2	4	4	3	4	3	4	3	4
4	4	4	5	2	3	3	3	5	5	5	5	3	3	3	3
2	2	5	3	5	4	5	5	5	5	5	5	3	3	4	4
2	3	5	4	3	4	3	5	5	5	5	5	4	3	4	3
2	3	4	4	4	5	4	4	3	4	3	3	3	3	4	4

P1. Business	P2. Agriculture	P3. Social
1 Lectures	**1 Reference Study**	**1 Official discussions**
Listen for overall	Intensive for all infm	Reading forms
Comprehension	Specific assignments	Complete documents
Make notes	Evaluative reading	Discuss with officials
Ask for clarification	Main infm rdg	
2 Seminars/Tutorials	**2 Current Literature**	**2 Social in Britain**
Discuss given topics	Routine check	Personal information
Listen for comprehension	Keep abreast	Invitations
Make notes	For main information	Mealtime conversation
Ask for clarification		Complaints
		Polite conversation
3 Reference Study	**3 English lessons**	**3 Places of Interest**
Intensive reading	Test study	Reading text for infm
Reading for main infm	Teacher exposition	Entrance/tickets
Assignment rdg	Group work	Guidebooks
Assessment rdg		Listen to commentary
		Ask for information
4 Writing Reports	**4 Other**	**4 Shopping**
Sort out information	(Note: English is not	Attract attention
Factual writing	much used in this	Discuss goods
Evaluative writing	Spanish context,	Give choice
	outside the study area)	Arr payment
		Complaints
		Sale documents
5 Keeping up-to-date		**5 Health**
Routine checking		Appt-person/phone
Reading for intensive		Discuss symptoms
Reading for infm search		Complete forms
		Medical directions
6 Indust/Comm Visits		**6 Restaurants/cafes**
Discuss topics		Attract attention
Discuss after visit		Place order(s)
Listening for infm		Deal with bill
Take notes		Complaints
Ask for clarification		
		7 Travel
		Timetables, schedules
		State destination
		Pay fares
		Maps, explanations
		Road signs/symbols

P4. Engineering	P5. Technician	P6. Medicine
1 Lectures	**1 Lectures**	**1 Diagnosis**
Work sheets	Listen to explanations	Questioning,
Notes/diagrams	Listen to instructions	rephrasing
Displays/models	Coord with colleagues	Compr garbled infm
Seek description	Take notes	Notes for records
Understand lectures	Record test results	Ask for clarification
	Questions & comments	
	Read instr for test	
	Read instr re specimen	
2 Tutorials	**2 Reference Study**	**2 Instruct Staff**
Sheets, notes, displays		Groups or individuals
Seek clarification		Question to check
Evaluate schemes	Rdg for main information	Write notes (med codes)
Problem solving	Intensive reading	Requests re instructions
Mathematical probs	Take notes	
Assignment apprec		
3 Experiments	**3 Give Recommendations**	**3 Write**
Prove hypothesis	Prepare notes	Personal letters
Solve problems	Speak to notes	Case descriptions
Write up experiments	Talk about diagrams	Note form
Report on projects	Answer queries	Full reports
Explore principles		
4 Reference Study	**4 Self-Access**	**4 Students Seminars**
		(conduct)
Intensive experiments	Tape-slide uses	Explain themes
Intensive re applics	Reading for main infm	Question, correct
Refer to tables, data	Intensive reading	Present peer seminars
Subject periodicals		Notes, handouts
		Blackboard, OHP
5 Field Work		**5 Attend Less/Seminars**
General site visit		Comprehend overall
Periodical work visits		Selective retention
Survey instruments		Notes for reconstruct
Experimental surveys		Ask for clarification
Discuss problems		Present own topic
Write up experiments		Informal discussions
		6 Reference Study
		Intensive reading for all
		Reading for main point
		Reading for spec. assignment
		Assess position
		Routine check
		Exophoric reading

(This list gives the superordinate terms and the 'P' profiles which indicate their significance eg 4, 5, 6, indicates that P4, P5 and P6 record this tone)

Superordinate polarity	'P' occurrences
Happy - unhappy	6
Contented - discontented	5 5
*Pleasant(ing) - unpleasant(ing)	1 1 4 4 5 5 5 6
Cheerful - dejected	6 6
Frivolous - serious	5 5 5 6
Rejoicing - lamenting	6
Entertaining - tedious	4 5 5^h
Exciting - unexciting	5
Humorous - humourless	5 5 6 6
Sensitive - insensitive	4 4 6 6
Hoping - hopeless	4 5 6 6
Courageous - fearing	6
*Cautious - incautious	1 1 2 4 4 4 4 4 5 6 6
*Caring - indifferent	1 1 2 4 4 4 4 5 6
Wondering - unastonished	6 6
Modest - proud	5 5 5
*Formal - informal	1 1 1 2 4 4 4 4 5 5 5^h 6 6 6
Friendly - unfriendly	5 6 6
Courteous - discourteous	1 1 4 5^h
Sociable - unsociable	6
Unresentful - resentful	6
Pleased - displeased	6 6
Patient - impatient	1 6
*Grateful - ungrateful	1 4 4 5 6
*Honest - dishonest	1 1 2 4 6 6
*Disinterested - biased	1 1 1 2 5 6
*Respectful - disrespectful	1 4 4 4 4 5^h 6 6
Admiring - contemptuous	5
Praising - detracting	1 5 6
*Approving - disapproving	1 1 1 2 4 5 6 6
Regretting - unregretting	5^h 6
Temperate - intemperate	6 6
Excitable - unexcitable	6 6
Willing - unwilling	1 1 4 4 6 6 6
Resolute - irresolute	4 6 6 6
*Inducive - dissuasive	1 1 1 2 5 6 6
Active - inactive	1 1 4 6 6 6
Concordant - discordant	1 1 1 2 6
Authoritative - unauthoritative	1 1 1 2 6 6
Compelling - uncompelling	1 1 1
*Certain - uncertain	1 1 1 2 4 5 5 6 6 6
*Intelligent - unintelligent	1 1 1^h 2 5 5 5^h 6 6
*Assenting - dissenting	1 1 1 2 4 5 5 6

Notes   (1)   P3. (Social English) has been omitted from this list
         (2)   The symbol ^{h} denotes a hyponym
         (3)   Tones used by 4 or more of the 5 profiles are indicated with an asterisk.

Inventory of Language Skills

We now record which Profiles require the Language Skills of the Munby list, to which refer for expansion of the abbreviated titles below. Skills required by 4 or more profiles (out of 6) are marked with an asterisk.

Skill Category   **Abbreviated title**

1   Discriminating sounds in isolated words.

                                                     nil

2   Articulating sounds in isolated words.

                                                     nil

3   Discriminating sounds in connected speech.

     3.1   Strong/weak forms   4

4   Articulating sounds in connected speech.

4.1	Strong/Weak forms	4 5 6
4.2	Neutralisation	5
4.3	Reduction vowels	5
4.4	Sound modification	5
4.5	Word boundaries	5 6
4.6	Allophonic variation	5 6

5   Discriminating stress within words.

5.1	Accentual patterns	5
5.2	Meaningful patterns	5
5.3	Compounds	5

6   Articulating stress within words.

6.1	Accentual patterns	5 6
6.2	Meaningful patterns	5 6
6.3	Compounds	5 6

7   Recognising stress variations in connected speech.

7.2	Meaningful prominence	3 4 6

15   Interpreting attitudinal meaning.

    15.1   Pitch height   1 3
    15.2   Pitch range   1 3 4
    15.3   Pause   1 3
    15.4   Tempo   1 3

16   Expressing attitudinal meaning.

    16.1-4   as for last drill   4 6

17   Reorganising the script.

    17.1   Graphemes   3 5 6
  *17.2   Spelling   3 4 5 6
    17.3   Punctuation   3 5 6

18   Manipulating the script.

    18.1   Graphemes   3 5 6
  *18.2   Spelling   3 4 5 6
    18.3   Punctuation   3 6

19   Deducing meaning of unfamiliar lexical items.

    19.1.1   Stress, roots   1 2 4
    19.1.2   Affixation   1 2
    19.1.3   Derivation   1 4
    19.1.4   Compounding   1 4
    19.2   Contextual clues   1 2 3

*20   Understanding explicitly stated information.

    1 2 3 4 6

*21   Expressing information explicitly.

    1 3 4 5 6

22   Understanding information not explicit.

  *22.1   Inferences   1 2 3 6
    22.2   Figurative language   3 6

23 Expressing information implicitly.

    23.1   Inference   6
    23.2   Figurative lang   6

24 Understanding conceptual meaning.

*24.1	Quantity	1	2	3	4	5	6
*24.2	Definiteness	1	2		4		6
*24.3	Comparison	1	2	3	4		6
*24.4	Time	1	2		4	5	6
*24.5	Location	1	2		4		6
*24.6	Means	1	2		4	5	6
*24.7	Cause, etc	1	2		4		6

25 Expressing conceptual meaning.

*25.1	Quantity	1		4	5	6
*25.2	Definiteness	1		4	5	6
*25.3	Comparison	1		4	5	6
*25.4	Time	1	3	4	5	6
*25.5	Location	1	3	4	5	6
*25.6	Means	1		4	5	6
*25.7	Cause, etc	1	3	4	5	6

26 Understanding communicative value (re context)

*26.1	With indicators	1	2	3	6
*26.2	Without indicators	1	2	3	6

27 Expressing communicative value

*27.1	With indicators	1	3	5	6
27.2	Without indicators	1		5	6

28 Understanding relations within sentence

28.1	Structure elements			3	5
*28.2.1	Premodification	1	2	3	5
*28.2.2	Postmodification	1	2	3	5
*28.2.3	Disjuncts	1	2	3	5
28.3	Negation			3	5	6
28.4	Modal auxiliaries		2	3	5
28.5	Connectors		2	3	5
28.6-7	Embedding + theme		2	3	5

29   Expressing relations within sentence.

29.1	Structure elements	3 5 6
*29.2.1	Premodifications	1 3 5 6
*29.2.2	Postmodifications	1 3 5 6
*29.2.3	Disjuncts	1 3 5 6
29.3	Negation	3 5 6
29.4	Modal auxiliaries	3 5
29.5	Connectors	5 6
29.6	Complex embedding	1 6
29.7	Focus + theme	6

30   Understanding lexical cohesion devices.

30.1	Repetition	3 6
30.2	Synonomy	2 3 6
30.3	Hyponomy	2 6
30.4	Antithesis	2 6
30.5	Apposition	3 6
30.6	Set/collocation	1 6
30.7	General Words	2 3 6

31   Using lexical cohesion devices.

31.1	Repetition	3 6
31.2	Synonomy	1 6
31.3	Hyponomy	1 6
31.4	Antithesis	6
31.5	Apposition	6
31.6	Set/collocation	1 3 6
31.7	General words	2 3 6

32   Understanding grammatical cohesion devices.

*32.1	Reference (c+a)	1 2 3 4
32.2	Comparison	2
32.3	Substitution	1 2
32.4	Ellipsis	1 2 3
32.5	Time/place relaters	2 3
32.6	Logical connectors	1 2 3

33   Using grammatical cohesion devices.

33.1	Reference	1 3 6
33.2	Comparison	6
33.3	Substitution	1 6
33.4	Ellipsis	1 6
33.5	Time/place relaters	1 3 6
33.6	Logical connectors	1 3 4

34   Interpreting text by going outside

34.1	Exophoric reference	1 3
34.2	'Between lines'	1 3
34.3	Own experience	1 2

35   Recognising indicators

*35.1	Introduce idea	2 3 5 6
35.2	Develop idea	2 3 6
35.3	Transition	1 3 6
35.4	Concluding	3 6
35.5	Emphasis	2 5 6
35.6	Clarification	3 6
*35.7	Anticipation	1 2 3 6

36   Using indicators.

36.1	Introduce idea	3
36.2	Develop idea	1
36.3	Transition	1
36.4	Concluding	1
36.5	Emphasis	3
36.6	Clarification	6
36.7	Anticipation	1 3

37   Identifying main/important point.

37.1	Vocal underlining	1 3
37.2	End-focus	-
37.3	Verbal clues	1 3
37.4	Topic sentence	1 2 6

38   Indicating main/important point.

    38.1   Vocal underlining   3
    38.2   End-focus   -
    38.3   Verbal clues   1 3 6
    38.4   Topic sentence   6

39   Distinguishing main idea by differentiation.

    39.1   Primary/secondary   2 4 5
   *39.2   Whole/parts   1 2 4 5
    39.3   Process/stages   2 4 5
    39.4   Category/exponent   2 5
    39.5   Statement/example   2 5
    39.6   Fact/opinion   1 2 5
    39.7   Proposition/argument   1 2 5

40   Extracting salient points to summarise.

    40.1   Whole text   1 2 5
    40.2   Idea   1 2 5
    40.3   Underlying point   1 5

41   Extracting relevant points re.

   *41.1   Coordination   1 2 5 6
    41.2   Rearrangement   1 6
   *41.3   Tabulation   1 2 4 6

42   Expanding salient points into.

    42.1   Whole text summary   1
    42.2   Topic summary   1

43   Reducing text through rejection of.

    43.1   Systemic items   6
    43.2   Repetition etc.   6
    43.4   Example compressions   6
    43.5   Abbreviations   1 2 6
   *43.6   Symbols   1 2 4 6

44 Basic reference skills.

*44.1	Layout	1 2 3 4 5 6
*44.2	Tables, indices	2 3 4 6
44.3	Cross-reference	4 6
44.4	Catalogues	1 6
44.5	Phonetic transcriptions	6

45 Skimming to obtain.

45.1	Gist	1 2 6
45.2	Impression	1 6

46 Scanning to locate.

46.1	Simple search (single)	3 6
46.2	Complex (single)	2 6
46.3	Simple (more than 1)	6
46.4	Complex (more than 1)	1 2 6
46.5	Whole topic	1 2 6

47 Initiating a discourse.

*47.1	Initiate	1 3 5 6
47.2	Introduce new	6
47.3	Introduce topic	6

48 Maintaining a discourse.

*48.1	Respond	1 3 5 6
48.2	Continue	1 5
48.3	Adopt	1 3 5
48.4	Interrupt	1 3
48.5	Mark time	1

49 Terminating a discourse.

49.1	Boundaries	-
49.2	Excuse	1 3
49.3	Conclude	3

50   Planning and organising discourse (rhetorically)

50.1	Definition	1	4		
*50.2	Classification	1	4	5	6
*50.3	Properties	1	4	5	6
*50.4	Process	1	4	5	6
*50.5	Change of state	1	4	5	6

51   Transcoding information from diagrams.

*51.1	Conversion into sp/wr.	1	3	4	5	6
*51.2	Comparison in sp/wr.	1	2	5	6	

52   Transcoding information from sp/wr.

*52.1	Completing a diagram	1	4	5	6
*52.2	Constructing diagrams	1	4	5	6

53   Recording information.

Nil

54   Relaying information.

54.1	Directly	3	5
54.2	Indirectly	3	4

Spec. 10   List of Micro-Functions

Include all micro-fuctions from each of the Scales 1-6 for educational/training purposes, and micro-functions from Scale 7 for social survival purposes. Functions to amplify content of Language Skill Number 26.

1   Scale of Certainty

Affirmation, certainty, probability, possibility, nil certainty and negation. Conviction, conjecture, doubt and disbelief.

2   Scale of Commitment

Intention and obligation.

3   Scale of Judgement

Valuation, verdiction, approval and disapproval.

4   Scale of Suasion

Inducement, compulsion, prediction and tolerance.

5   Argument

Information, agreement, disagreement and concession.

6   Rational Enquiry

Proposition, substantiation, supposition, implication, interpretation and classification.

7   Formulaic Communication

Greeting, farewell, acknowledgement, thanks, apology, good wishes, condolence, attention signals.

TWENTY IMPORTANT STUDENT CATEGORIES

Rank order	Programme	% of Participants	% Cumulative
1	Agriculture (incl. Fisheries, Timber, Vets)	17	
2	Engineering (excl. Agricultural Engineering)	13	
3	Medical (including Dental & Paramedics)	10	40%
4	Economics and Development	8	
5	Administration (Public)	7	
6	Education (+ Education Administration)	5	60%
7	English Teaching	5	
8	Mining & Geology	4	
9	Accountancy, Banking and Insurance	4	
10	Sciences	4	
11	Physical Planning	4	
12	Sociology	3	81%
13	Business Admin, Management & Marketing	3	
14	Media	3	
15	Industrials	2	
16	Statistics, Demography	2	
17	Transport	2	
18	Aviation	2	
19	Laws	1	
20	Marine Engineering, Ports, Harbours	1	100%

Appendix C

Acknowledgements to staff assisting in
preparation of specifications

Thanks are given to the following staff members who prepared participant specifications:

P.1.	Business Studies	Roger Hawkey
P.2.	Agricultural Science	John Munby
P. 3.	Social Survival	Shelagh Rixon
P. 4.	Civil Engineering	Melvin Hughes
P. 5.	Laboratory Technician	David Herbert
P. 6.	Medicine	Elizabeth Smyth

The major contribution to the operation has been John Munby's thesis, 'Specifying communicative competence; a sociolinguistic model for syllabus design,' shortly to be published by CUP[1]

Controller and Deputy Controller, English Language Division have also given advice on the requirements of the English Language Testing Service.

Directors ETIC and ELTI are thanked for allowing us to use staff for the specifications.

---

[1] Munby, John. *Communicative syllabus design.* CUP, 1978.

Appendix D

A statement of abilities required of first year entrants (Engineering Science) into Northern Universities (Joint Matriculation Board)

1   Knowledge and understanding of:

Terms, conventions and units commonly used in engineering science

Particular principles (or laws) and generalisations of engineering science, and their effects and interrelationships

Specialist apparatus and techniques used for the demonstration of the principles referred to above, and the limitations of such apparatus and techniques

The use of different types of apparatus and techniques in the solution of engineering problems

2   Abilities

Understand and interpret scientific and other information presented verbally, mathematically, graphically and by drawing

Appreciate the amount of information required to solve a particular problem

Understand how the main facts, generalisations and theories of engineering science can provide explanations of familiar phenomena

Recognise the scope, specification and requirements of a problem

Understand the operation and use of scientific apparatus and equipment

Recognise the analogue of a problem in related fields of engineering science and practice

3   Ability: Communication

Explain principles, phenomena, problems and applications adequately in simple English

Formulate relationships in verbal, mathematical, graphical or diagrammatic terms

Translate information from one form to another

Present the results of practical work in the form of reports which are complete, readily understandable and objective

4   Ability: Analysis

Break down a problem into its separate parts

Recognise unstated assumptions

Acquire, select and apply known information, laws and principles to routine problems and to unfamiliar problems, or those presented in a novel manner

5   Ability: Synthesis and Design

Design the manner in which an optimum solution may be obtained and to propose, where necessary, alternative solutions

Make a formal specification of a design or scheme

Make a plan for the execution or manufacture of the design or scheme

Use observations to make generalisations or formulate hypotheses

Suggest new questions and predictions which arise from these hypotheses

Suggest methods of testing these questions and predictions

6   Ability: Evaluation and Judgement

Check that hypotheses are consistent with given information, to recognise the significance of unstated assumptions, and to discriminate between hypotheses

Assess the validity and accuracy of data, observations, statements and conclusions

Assess the design of apparatus or equipment in terms of the results obtained and the effect upon the environment and suggest means of improvement

Judge the relative importance of all the factors that comprise an engineering situation

Appreciate the significance of social, economic, or design considerations in an engineering situation.

REACTION TO THE CARROLL PAPER (1)
Caroline M Clapham, University of Lancaster

The Carroll report states that the Davies Test (EPTB) is now unsatisfactory because:

1 It was not designed to cope with the number of students and diversity of courses that there are today

2 Many students fail to finish their courses because their English is not good enough

3 The emphasis in language teaching and testing has changed from an atomistic approach to a broader sociolinguistic one

4 The advent of ESP has led to fewer teachers and testers working towards the needs of all language users.

I am not sure whether 1 matters much for a test of the Davies kind and I know too little about the test's concurrent and predictive validity to comment on 2. However, a combination of 3 and 4 has led to such a drop in ithe test's face validity that it is losing the confidence of its users and will probably have to be changed. (Whatever Palmer and Bachman may think, face validity is of the utmost importance when a test is administered by non-statistically minded bodies.)

I should have liked to have been able to discuss the differences in content between the Davies Test and the proposed replacement, ELTS, but in his *Specifications* Carroll does not go so far as to describe the items in any detail. I can only, therefore, comment on some of the issues that lie behind them.

ELTS, as reported in these specifications, is planned to be radically different from the Davies Test, and I am rather alarmed by the number of changes envisaged. The proposals follow three swings of the pendulum of language teaching and testing theory: the new test is to test communicative competence, it is to be divided into different modules to test ESP, *and* it is to be criterion rather than norm referenced. There are very good arguments for all of these, but, since none of the three is yet well tried and tested, I wonder if it is wise to go for all of them at the same moment.

Even if we accept the arguments for the first two, what about the move to criterion referencing? At the present state of our knowledge, is this practicable, and is it in any case necessary?

Criterion Referenced Tests

To take the question of practicability first: for a criterion referenced test to work it must have a comprehensive list of language objectives to which it can be tied, and it must also be capable of being pretested to see whether each item tests the criterion in such a way that those who know it pass, and those who do not, fail. Carroll tackles the first of these very thoroughly — one of the main aims of his *Specifications* is to present a list of language objectives — but what about the pretesting? How, for example, should the proposed 250 multiple choice items be analysed? Traditional item analysis is, of course, norm referenced, with items being assessed according to a comparison of the reactions they elicit from high and low ranking students. In criterion referenced testing, though, the ranking of students is, by definition, irrelevant. Testers are not interested in whether more students at the top than at the bottom get an item right. They want to know whether those who know the subject, and those who do not, pass or fail accordingly. It may well be that since items also have to be checked for level and ambiguity, some sort of initial norm referenced analysis will have to be used, but what should happen after that?

Carroll treats this problem very lightly. He implies that since the aim will be to match students with their language requirements rather than with their fellows, representative samples will not be needed for the test preparation. The implication seems to be that norm-referenced tests need to be tried out on representative samples but that criterion-referenced ones do not. Carroll specifically says that once the communicative demands are defined, it is the test's job to decide how a particular candidate measures up to them, not to see how 'performance characteristics are distributed throughout a population of applicants . . .' He seems to be confusing the preparation of the test with its final administration. If a validated test is criterion-referenced, each candidate's performance will of course be compared with the language specification and not with that of other examinees, but before that stage is reached, the test **must** in some way be tried out on representative samples for level, reliability and validity. (Confusingly, Carroll does say in direct opposition to what he says elsewhere, that, 'our performance standards will derive from ongoing courses and their students'.)

Since there are these problems of construction, does this proficiency test need to be criterion referenced? I agree that a student's level of English should be compared with the level he needs for his course rather than with that of the other candidates (it would make no sense for a proficiency test to pass people according to percentiles, as it is rumoured some O and A Level boards do) but with a proficiency test, is such a fine diagnostic tool needed? Would not a norm-referenced test with set, validated target levels for each subtest, serve the purpose as well? As Carroll proposes, the marks in each language area could be set differently for the different disciplines and course demands, and the final score sheet could provide all the information described. I do not want to stray further into the marking system just yet, but I do want to question the necessity of embarking on the ill comprehended area of criterion referenced testing for proficiency, when there are at hand hardy statistical methods for norm referenced tests.[1]

The profiles

If a test is to be criterion referenced (and indeed preferably when it is not), there needs to be an adequate specification of the candidate's language requirements, and this specification is, of course, the nub of the Carroll report.

I shall not comment on the coverage, applicability and feasibility of these specification criteria in language learning and use, since they are based on John Munby's description of communicative needs (Munby, 1978). What I shall do is look at the manner in which they are used here. However, before I do that I must say something about the six profiles described in the report. I should have liked to have seen how much they helped to straighten the tester's muddled way through communicative competence and ESP, but unfortunately I cannot do this, as their use here is vitiated by the fact that five of them seem to have been invented by their compilers. Carroll gives reasons for this and I can see that 'comprehensive observational studies of the participants' would have been very time consuming. However, without such studies, surely the profiles are almost useless. Although Carroll points out that the field work depends too much on the subjective judgement of the compilers, he still draws conclusions from it. For example, he says that the profiles will be used to identify common areas, and areas of specific need on which diversified tests can be based. Indeed, most of his findings throughout the report, for example target levels of courses, variation in demand between different disciplines, and extraction of factors, are based on this

---

[1] Since preparing his *Specifications* Carroll seems to have tempered his views on criterion referenced testing. In Carroll 1980, page 10, he says 'Emphasis on the pre-specification of communicative tasks lends itself to criterion referenced techniques, but it is far too early to consider dispensing with the elaborate and well worked-out procedures of norm-based statistics.'

'data', and cannot therefore be trusted. This is a pity, because it is an excellent way of setting out the demands of different courses in a tangible and comparable way. In his explanation for collecting the data in this manner, Carroll rather startlingly says, 'The ultimate validation of our methods would be the effectiveness of the test based on their results.' To spend time constructing tests according to possibly false data would seem a waste of time; and if the tests were invalid, how would one know whether the data or poor test construction was at fault?

Even if the profiles were not just the result of educated guesses they would have been of little use because they are 'personalised' in order to 'counteract the natural but dangerous tendency to overgeneralise about communicative needs'. Unfortunately, this personalisation, far from counteracting it, actually encourages overgeneralisation. Nothing can prevent the reader, or indeed the writer, from treating the profiles as typical. That Carroll himself is misled is shown when he says that the first necessity is to study the needs of 'a typical student'.

The specifications

For the purposes of testing, the specifications fall into four categories:

Cat. 1 : Spec. 0	Student's background
Cat. 2 : Spec. 1, 2, 3, 4, 5, 7	Setting
Cat. 3 : Spec. 8, 9, 10	Manipulation of Language
Cat. 4 : Spec. 6	Target levels

Cat. 1 Carroll's argument is that the candidate is to be matched with his language requirements regardless of his background. In this case, age, mother tongue and previous English knowledge are strictly irrelevant. (This, of course, ignores the use of contrastive analysis in ESP testing.)

Cat. 2 and 3 These two categories form the basis for the criterion referenced list of objectives mentioned earlier, and had the profiles been based on solid research, would have provided the raw material from which a test such as ELTS could be constructed. There is obviously little point in looking at the substance of these profiles here, but I had hoped that we might be able to see how such material would be transformed into test items. Unfortunately, though, the report does not takes us to this stage.

If they were well researched, categories 2 and 3 would also provide invaluable evidence for or against the shift to ESP. Research is urgently needed into whether an ESP proficiency test is actually necessary, as the preparation of parallel ESP modules makes the construction of a valid and equitable test time consuming and difficult.

Cat. 4 With specification 6, target levels, we come on to marking, and a host of unsolved problems, of which the two most important are:

a) How does one set reliable and valid target levels?
b) How does one marry these up with reliable test scores?

Munby's target level specification consists of a two dimensional matrix giving size, complexity, range, delicacy, speed and flexibility by verbal medium, with levels ranging from 1 to 7 (see *Specifications* Appendix). This is set beside a tolerance matrix giving error, style, reference, repetition and hesitancy by verbal medium, with levels ranging from 1 to 5. When he introduces them, Carroll uses Munby's scales, but in his succeeding discussion converts the 7-point scale to percentages, for, he says, comparative purposes. This seems to me to be unnecessary since two 7-point scales can easily be compared, and it is also dangerous as it makes the scale look deceptively equal interval. Indeed Carroll seems to treat it as such, for he has worked out means on the strength of it.

Here again the inadequacy of the data means we can make no deductions about comparative levels of course demands, but we can look at how the system might work. Presumably the plan is that the testing staff would fill in the course target levels after consultation with instructors and heads of departments. It is an attractive scheme, but I doubt whether there would ever be enough time for it to be implemented, especially since it would need frequent updating as course demands changed. I doubt too, whether many heads of departments would want to be so involved. In practice, time constraints would probably prevent the matrices being used, and test compilers would be happy if they were able to get amalgamated listening, reading, speaking and writing levels.

Of course, whether the levels are simple or complicated the same problem remains: how can they be made valid and reliable? The report admits that the profile levels it gives may not be reliable, but it does not say how they could be made so.

It is also not clear from the report how Carroll intends to use the tolerance levels since they are not included in the marking scheme graph. Although the idea of tolerance levels is very appealing, I wonder how much they would improve the precision of the results. Since the target and tolerance levels are based on different scales it is difficult to compare the two, but if research bore out Carroll's statement that tolerance ratings are negatively correlated with level of demand, and if this correlation was a high one, then tolerance might well be omitted. Certainly the marking system would be much easier if tolerance could be left out.

Setting the target levels is hard enough, but matching these with test results is even harder. If the whole test was subjectively scored according to the same 7-point scale, it might be possible for both setters and markers to determine their levels in the same way, though even here, decisions would have to be made about such questions as how much flexibility to allow. (I am not sure, for example, where Carroll's four point error comes from, nor what his 'significantly above the level' means.) Once there is a multiple choice element in the test, the difficulty is compounded; there would **have** to be many trials of the test, and the results would **have** to be correlated with students' actual abilities and with the target levels. This would take time, and would lead to all the usual validation problems, but it would be absolutely essential if the test was to be fair both to the prospective departments, and to the students whose careers were at stake.

Test Design

The mention of multiple choice questions brings me to the proposed test format, and it is surely only once we have a detailed idea of what this will be that we can know whether the *Specifications* are indeed the breakthrough in test design that the author claims. It is only once we see how they can be applied that we can know whether the ensuing battery will have face, content and construct validity. Alas, the report stops here. It does give a bare outline of the proposed test, listing the number of items and areas to be tested, but it does not describe the items in any detail. All it says, tantalisingly, is that 'in our preparatory work, we have had no difficulty in devising test types to measure the varied communicative features revealed in the specifications . .'

Finale

The Carroll report makes far-reaching suggestions for changes in proficiency testing, and by providing a concrete plan for people to criticise, should advance our knowledge of how to test communicative competence. However, a very great deal of research will have to be carried out before a reputable international test can be based on it.

BIBLIOGRAPHY

CARROLL, B J
  Testing Communicative Performance. Pergamon Institute of English. 1980.

MUNBY, JOHN
  Communicative Syllabus Design. Cambridge University Press. 1978.

REACTION TO THE CARROLL PAPER (2)

Clive Criper, University of Edinburgh

The stated aim of the English Language Testing Service (ELTS) as set out in these specifications is quite clear. It is:

1 to test whether any student is already able to cope with the language needs of his academic course;

2 to assess the nature and duration of any language tuition that a student might need to bring himself up to the level at which he could cope with his academic course.

What is claimed to be new in ELTS is a matching of course requirements with the test instrument. ELTS is thus designed to be a model of a criterion-referenced test where the criterion is based on a close analysis of the real communicative needs of a student attending a particular course.

I think there can be no disagreement with these basic aims. They are aims which we can applaud without reservation and indeed feel virtuous that we have taken the path of righteousness.

Reality, unfortunately, cannot be kept entirely out of sight and out of mind as one reads the apparent basis for the ELTS test — at any rate as specified by Brendan Carroll in his paper. Let me take in turn some areas in which reality and ELTS ideology appear to be in conflict.

Communicative Needs of the Users

The whole argument against the use of general proficiency type tests for use as placing tests for Higher Education students rests on our ability to identify different student's needs. This is clearly the crux of the argument of the paper by Brendan Carroll and a large proportion of the paper appears to be spent on 'proving' this fact. The 'proof' offered, if it is meant as a proof rather than a statement of belief, is highly spurious.

ELTS Argument

The basic starting point of Brendan Carroll's work was Munby's needs analysis. Without commenting on Munby's thesis as such, it will suffice to say that Carroll follows the outline of Munby's specification parameters. These are a set of typologies which are meant to cover all the important linguistic

117

and social areas which might affect the language to be used in any particular situation. Each typology then divides up the world into a number of discrete categories against which a student's needs for English are matched.

In the present instance this kind of matching has been carried out for six 'students', the majority of whom, it appears, are imaginary. The needs have been analysed on an intuitive basis by staff who have some knowledge of the subject area.

When it comes to specifying the proficiency target levels in each of the four skills a numerical figure is given on a subjective basis. Notwithstanding the disclaimer, **these figures are then used as if they are genuine experimental figures on a true equal interval scale.** Scores are added and averaged, and are treated as being on an equal interval scale from which conclusions can be drawn about the length of study necessary to reach a certain level.

In another area — that of the 'Essential Language Skill Categories', a further quantitative comparison is made between the six subjects and the same spurious 'proof' of connection between various of the subjects is made.

There are other areas of the specification parameters, eg microfunctions, where much of the theoretical basis of the specification might be challenged and, inevitably, many areas where one could argue at length about the rating of needs provided by the analysts. Such arguments would only be of interest, however, in showing that the analysis made is essentially a theoretical one and not an experimental one.

Course Requirements

There is an unstated assumption in the whole paper that individuals picked out for illustration of the scheme are going to institutions which are sufficiently similar for generalisations to be made about the communicative needs of their students. The ideology of the ELTS scheme requires a close matching between student and institution.

I am extremely doubtful whether the language needs of students going to do postgraduate work in Agriculture, for example, have more in common than between some students doing, say, Medicine and Engineering. If one tries to specify the content of lectures in Engineering, it becomes apparent that the individual variation in lecturers, techniques and approaches outweighs anything that the content may have in common.

In addition, as Carroll rightly points out, Universities and other institutions in the UK have considerable autonomy. Within most institutions there is also considerable variation in Faculty policies and, even more importantly, in departmental policies. It is also true that individual Supervisors within the same department have very different views of the minimum level of English that they require from overseas students. This latter fact of life has, in the past, been one of the major reasons why Universities have found it an impossible task to specify clear-cut language requirements for their post-graduate students.

The implication of this is two-fold. Firstly it will never be possible to specify in detail the requirements in the various skills for a particular group of subjects across all Universities. Testing Centres, such as the British Council overseas offices, will not be able to match institutions' profiles very closely. It follows that, secondly, a fine assessment of needs, in test terms, will be wasted.

Practical Considerations

There are three main areas to be considered — testing centres, particularly overseas, the UK 'customer', be it University or Technical College or hospital and the test producer.

Test Producer — Reference has already been made to the difficulty of pro-ducing reliable generalisable 'profiles of needs' except where there are gross differences. Leaving aside any argument about the ease or difficulty in design-ing test items to cover the 'specification parameters', a major problem comes up in the plan to use subject tests, eg reading comprehension using specific subject area texts. While such a procedure appeals to common sense and thus has great face validity there are at least two types of difficulty.

Firstly, the subject specialist, whether testee or teacher, tends to require more and more specialist texts. To the specialist there is no such thing as an 'agri-cultural' text covering all related branches of the subject, any more than there is a 'medical' text. The idea of a 'special purpose' text for a wide range of sub-disciplines is contradictory and paradoxically may potentially be more sub-ject to criticism on the grounds of non-validity than a more general text.

Secondly, it may be more difficult to control the texts for background knowledge of the testees. Background or factual knowledge is an enormous advantage in answering comprehension questions. While it may be argued that there is a certain basic minimum knowledge that can be expected of any student in a particular subject, in practice no such minimum knowledge exists, both because of the educational and cultural background of different students and because of the existence of a multitude of sub-disciplinary back-grounds that students may have. A language test as such cannot afford to be seen to be classifying students according to their subject knowledge rather than their language ability, otherwise receiving institutions may come to reject its use.

Testing Centres - Carroll makes reference, quite rightly, to the importance of cost and time that would be involved in the ELTS overseas and states that there is a need for a quick screening test. In any overall assessment of ELTS I think that the time/money cost has to be weighed very carefully against the extra information which a test based on an assessment of projected communicative needs requires. This is particularly so if the testing centres will not, in practice, have the information about the real requirements of the receiving institutions. Considerable judgement will also be required to make recommendations on the basis of the test and the way that the Davies test has sometimes been administered and interpreted leaves one with considerable doubts about using a far more sophisticated instrument.

UK Customers - My experience suggests that in Universities at least the level of sophistication in interpreting and using English test scores is very low indeed. At Edinburgh, two test scores are widely used, Davies (EPTB) and the English Language Battery (ELBA), and only a limited number of people understand what the somewhat odd figure of 'Davies 40' means, and the similar odd figures of 'ELBA 50 and 70'. Only the specialists have an idea of the relationship between the two. Considerable difficulties will inevitably arise in interpreting either scores or band scores for different skills and I fear that many institutions, or at any rate individuals within them, will operate on some rule-of-thumb averaging operation. If that happens, then the whole purpose of the ELTS 'profile' design will be vitiated.

Summary

The need 'to test whether a student is already able to cope with the language needs of his academic course', is crystal clear and happily the British Council has taken up the challenge. Carroll's 1978 presentation of the specifications for ELTS, aimed at testing a student's potential ability to operate in a study environment raises issues in testing as interesting and as problematic as those in the teaching of ESP. What will be needed will be a programme of development and validation over several years which will deal with the real world of testing and needs rather than the hypothetical constructs of Carroll out of Munby.

BACKGROUND TO THE SPECIFICATIONS FOR AN ENGLISH LANGUAGE TESTING SERVICE AND SUBSEQUENT DEVELOPMENTS

Ian Seaton, ELTSLU, The British Council, London

Consideration of Carroll's paper divorced from a knowledge of the context in which it was produced and the developments following its publication is problematic, since the questions 'What led to these specifications?' and 'What has been done or what is likely to be done about them?' recur in the reader's mind. The paper reproduced above represents but one phase, although a vital one, in the complex process of establishing the English Language Testing Service. No further information on the subsequent development of the service had been made public when the reactions to Carroll's paper were written. Some information on the background of ELTS and more recent developments is therefore given below to provide a context for the reactions and discussion.

In the latter half of the 1970's the British Council was faced with the need to introduce a new or modified English proficiency testing system geared to the changes in ELT developments, notably in ESP, and to the changes in the needs of sponsored students seeking to come to Britain. However, it was faced with two closely linked constraints — one professional, the other financial. The first was that even in January 1978 there was no body of research into the testing of ESP which could be drawn upon. English proficiency tests were being conducted for special groups at that time, but not on anything approaching the scale that the Council would be required to test. The major ESP test system established in Britain by then was the PLAB test administered by the General Medical Council, and some industrial companies had commissioned publishers or other groups to construct ESP tests for internal use in their own training programmes. But results of any research that may have been carried out on those tests had not been published. This contrasted sharply with the volume of research by Lado, J B Carroll and others that was available to the constructors of the TOEFL, EPTB, ELBA and other English proficiency tests more than 15 years previously. Secondly, the Council was entering a period of increasing financial stringency which precluded the possibility of commissioning elaborate in-depth research.

Nevertheless a decision was made in 1977 to commission six small teams of qualified teachers and consultants to devise the specifications that Carroll has reported. The teams chose to use the Communicative Needs Processor proposed by Munby (1978) to organise their survey and specifications.

Early in 1978 the recommendations of Carroll's report were accepted in principle and new teams drawn from the British Council English Language Division and the University of Cambridge Test Development and Research Unit edited the specifications further and produced items for a preliminary version of the test known as ELTS. This test observed the two phase (screening test and subject specific modules) system proposed by Carroll and was trialled in Britain later in the year. After analysis of the results, revisions were made and a second version pre-tested overseas in 1979. After further modifications a third version was produced and put into operation in a number of selected countries from early 1980. It can be seen that although the speed of introduction was carefully controlled, resources were fully committed and it was not possible to publish reports of the developments as they took place. However the *User Handbook* containing details on the nature of the test was published in late 1980, and the *Specialist Handbook* with technical details of the tests is scheduled for publication in late 1981. Details of the pretesting and analysis of the results will be abstracted from the handbook and published separately as a very brief report at the same time. Copies of these publications can be obtained from the British Council English Language Testing Liaison Unit or from the University of Cambridge Local Examinations Syndicate.

One of the latest and most important developments is that within the overall validation framework an extensive follow-up validation study of the test is being undertaken by the English Language Testing Service in cooperation with the Institute of Applied Language Studies, University of Edinburgh. This study should give information which will be valuable to the test consumers and which could well lead to modification of certain specifications or formats in the future.

REPORT OF THE DISCUSSION ON TESTING ENGLISH FOR SPECIFIC PURPOSES

J Charles Alderson, University of Lancaster

The purpose of the discussion was to consider the possibilities and problems of testing within an ESP framework, and not to focus on the English Language Testing Service recently established by the British Council and University of Cambridge Local Examinations Syndicate. However, to date almost no attention has been given within testing circles to the problems of ESP testing, so that one of the very few articles of relevance to the debate is the *Specifications for an English Language Testing Service,* written within the British Council by Brendan Carroll. In addition, the ELTS is one of very few cases so far in the United Kingdom of an attempt to carry out ESP testing. (One other case is the PLAB test of the General Medical Council.) Inevitably, therefore, much of the debate centred on the ELTS since it provides a practical example of the problems of ESP testing. For this debate, the *Specifications* document proved to be an excellent starting point, raising as it does so many issues, and attempting to introduce ideas into the field of testing from the 'outside' EFL/ESL world, as well as from applied linguistics. It should be remembered that this document was originally produced as a paper for discussion **before** the final specifications were worked out.

Proficiency versus Achievement

The discussion confined itself to the topic of proficiency testing for ESP. This was partly because the *Specifications* paper itself is concerned with proficiency testing, but more importantly because there is a sense in which the development of achievement tests of or for ESP simply does not present a problem. Any achievement test must crucially depend on its content. That is, to be valid, an achievement test must be based on the syllabus which has preceded it: otherwise it is by definition not an achievement test. Thus the validity problem of an achievement test is essentially a sampling problem. To the extent that it is possible to develop a syllabus for specific purposes, it is also possible to develop a specific purpose test, since it 'merely' has to reflect that syllabus. The problem of what an ESP syllabus looks like: what items, skills or content it contains, and how that content is determined (be it through prior needs analysis, negotiation with learners, fiat, or whatever), is simply not the concern of the constructors of achievement tests. Proficiency tests, on the other hand, are not based upon any particular syllabus, again by definition. One is, therefore, faced with the problem of deciding what must be tested.

The Need for Specific Tests

Once it was agreed that the discussion was properly concerned with proficiency tests, it was then necessary to clarify why proficiency tests should test ESP. The *Specifications* document suggests, in the Foreword, that it is necessary to 'specify the communication needs' of potential testees, because of the inadequacy of previous test instruments:

> 'there is always a number of students who have to abandon their studies and return home because of their language inadequacy and the progress of a much larger number is adversely affected in one way or another by language problems.'

Thus the *Specifications* document aims to explore 'ways of devising a more up-to-date system which will be able to cope with a problem of the size and diversity of which the earlier system had not been designed to meet'. Later it is made clear that the need is for tests 'which will cater more completely for the many different types of programme (of courses of study) we are testing for'. Thus, there is a need for a new test or series of tests because poor students are getting through, or rather the Davies test (EPTB) is failing to identify students who have problems, and it does not cater for the needs of a wide variety of students. Unfortunately we are not offered empirical evidence that the existing test has in fact failed to identify students with problems. Indeed it was suggested that it may be the case that 'poor' students are being accepted despite low EPTB scores, and that the problem is not so much the identification of weakness, but the lack of remedial action.

We are usefully given criteria by which a new instrument can be judged: it will identify such students, and it will meet the needs of that variety of students more adequately. However, it does not follow from the 'fact' that the existing instrument is deficient that what is needed is an ESP test, or a battery of specialist tests: one plausible solution might simply be a better general test, constructed along similar lines to existing instruments. The evidence suggests that different academic departments do indeed place different language demands upon overseas students. It is certainly plausible that an undergraduate course in Engineering will have different linguistic requirements from a postgraduate course in linguistics. It is not clear, however, that this implies the development of separate tests for Engineers and Linguists. Even if the activities they have to contend with are entirely dissimilar — for example, a taught course contrasted with a masters degree by dissertation alone — it does not follow that different tests of language ability are required. It could be that all that is needed is that different levels of proficiency are required for different subject disciplines. Thus, in order to succeed in Engineering, a.student 'needs' an EPTB score of, say, 36, whereas to succeed in Linguistics, a student 'needs' 42 on EPTB. Indeed, this is typically the way in which entry requirements have been varied for different disciplines, in the UK and in the US. It may be the case that separate tests are required, but we do not have satisfactory evidence yet that this is so.

One major argument advanced for specific tests is that of face validity: a test for Engineering students should look like a test for Engineering students and not like a test for Social Scientists, or worse, Generalists. There is a very real problem with face validity arguments of this kind which is related to the question: Suited for whom? Will all engineers — electronic, electrical, chemical, civil, mechanical — agree on the face validity of an Engineering test?

Perhaps the most powerful argument for specific tests is that of the diagnostic value of a profile of a student which can be matched against the communicative needs of his particular course of study. Regardless of the presence or absence of predictive validity of such a profile — predictive, that is, of final academic grades, or whatever — there is, or may be, value in profiles of students' abilities, relatable to institutional criteria, for both administrative purposes (that is, admission decisions) and for pedagogic purposes, since hopefully such information would allow remedial action to be taken on a language course, for example.

One further advantage of such a profile is that it might encourage people — institutions — to be explicit about what they want and expect students to be able to do (with language), if the students are to succeed. This, however, presupposes that it is actually possible for subject departments — or indeed, even applied linguists — actually to specify what the language-related requirements are. This may not be the case: it may be impossible both to determine what the linguistic demands being made on any individual actually will be, and, furthermore, it may be very difficult to specify in advance what difficulties a particular student will have in meeting those linguistic or language-related demands. Some students, it was argued, will learn to cope much more easily than others. Thus a proficiency test, which simply labels a student at one point in time, gives no information about learning potential, and for that very reason may be inadequate. Two students may achieve the same proficiency score, but have very different potential: one student may have greater aptitude or adaptability than the other, perhaps having learnt the foreign language for only six months, whilst the other has studied it for fifteen years: in such a case one might expect the student with the shorter learning history to have greater potential for coping in a foreign language environment. Thus, what may be needed is not only a proficiency test, but in addition an aptitude test, or an adaptability test, or details of individual learning histories.

The problem with predictive validity of any test is that so many variables enter into a student's ultimate performance, in addition to whatever the particular test is measuring, that one is unlikely to get higher validities for aptitude tests than for proficiency. This would be an argument against replacing proficiency tests with aptitude tests. The issue was raised of whether it is in any case the task of a language test, be it general or specific, to predict performance in, say, Physics. Might it not be perhaps less presumptuous and more valid, simply to require that a language test should predict how much a student will improve in language, and to what level? Thus what one needs to know is not to what extent EPTB or any other proficiency test correlates with academic performance, but to what extent it correlates with itself, or another 'relevant' measure of language ability, at course end, when final academic success is being judged. The diagnostic argument is that we need to be able to predict the difficulties students will have **because of** language: the crucial question is: Is this knowable? Be this as it may, existing tests are frequently used as if they were predictive of final academic success, or as if they predicted eventual language proficiency levels. EPTB scores, for example, are often interpreted as indicating a required number of weeks of English tuition before commencing academic study: a student achieving a score of 32 on EPTB may be expected to take a twelve week English course, whereas a student with a score of 36 might be required only to undergo six weeks. This is a misuse of the test score, because the test was not validated in such a way, and is in any case unintelligent because it ignores language learning history.

How Specific is Specific?

For the sake of the argument, it was assumed that specific tests are needed, that evidence is, or will one day be, available which indicates incontrovertibly and uncontroversially that a general test is simply not doing its job. (This assumption, it was noted, implies that we know what the job of a proficiency test is: that we can answer the question: Proficiency for What?)

The problem that was addressed was: how specific should a specific test be? Is it, in other words, possible to draw up a real specification for a language test? Carroll claims that the development of tests within ELTS represents 'a process of diversification of test instruments to meet the diversity of test situations'. The question that inevitably arose was: when are 'test situations' no longer diverse, but similar, or similar enough? The ultimate specification of a test situation must be that of one individual at one point in time: above that level, a claim of specificity must be invalid for some individual at some point in time. Yet it is in principle impossible to devise an instrument for one individual at one point in time, which is in any sense reliable and valid, since to determine the extent of such reliability and validity, one has to be able to compare performances on the same instrument. Thus, *a priori*, a specific test is impossible. However, it was felt that there may be practical reasons for constructing a 'more or less' specific test — a test for engineers or for chemical engineers, or for chemical engineers going to study at Lancaster. Nevertheless, it was pointed out, there are practical problems in matching specific students to tests. Which ELTS modular test, for example, out of the six presently available (Physical, Life, Social and Medical Sciences, Technology and General Academic) should be taken by a student of Urban and Regional Studies, whose course will include Law and Economics courses as well as courses in Technology? Should such a student take a General Academic test, (ie less specific), or should a test be developed for Urban and Regional Studies, (ie more specific)? What about the (frequent) cases of students who have a background in Physical Sciences, who are coming to the UK to do a (to them) novel course in Technology? Do they take the Physical Science test or the Technology test? It is not clear that any principled decision is possible, and if the tests are not comparable, then students suffer the luck of the draw. How is a student to decide which test to take? On what basis can he choose? How can a British Council English Language Officer advise him? The point is that the level of specificity chosen for the test is inevitably arbitary. One can attempt to analyse communicative needs — looking at study situations, for example — and then find what different study situations have in common. One thereby extracts the specific from specific situations, abstracting generalities in order to cover more situations. To what extent can such an endeavour be characterised as constructing an ESP test? Might it not be the case, as suggested in the discussion about communicative tests, that if one abstracts far enough, one might end up with linguistic proficiency or Grammar, as being common to all language-related situations?

Another problem frequently encountered with specific tests is that of previous knowledge of the subject matter; at what level of specificity or generality can one be relatively sure that one is not testing subject-matter knowledge rather than linguistic or communicative abilities? Can one (should one) be sure that prior (subject) knowledge will not give one candidate an advantage over another candidate? A related problem is that of lack of knowledge: a specific test might well assume or presuppose subject knowledge that the testees do not have; native-speaker A-level students might have such knowledge, and the text may be premissed upon that, but differences in educational and/or cultural backgrounds may mean that overseas students may not have the knowledge. Two questions arose: does it matter, since overseas students will in any case have to read texts premissed upon pre-existent knowledge, usually within an English-speaking community? And how can one possibly avoid involving prior knowledge, since comprehension and presumably production must depend upon the prior existence of some set of knowledge?

One might, if one were simply to characterise the tasks that students have to engage in their target situations, be able to specify a set of Study Skills which are common to study situations, and one might then attempt to measure such study skills in the proficiency tests. Such is, in effect, what the ELTS test is becoming. The question then is whether one actually needs a Munby-type specification at the level of microskills, of the sort advocated by Carroll, in order to arrive at a relevant set of study skills for inclusion in a language or study skills test. In fact, it is, as suggested already, probably impossible for an ELTS-type test to base itself on specifications of the type advocated in the document: the specifications are simply too specific, and certainly do not allow the generation of texts or text types. Criper has already mentioned the danger of specific texts: that they satisfy no-one because they are not specific enough. The fact is that the Communicative Needs Processor does not help one to select texts or items for a test.

The point of the specification of microskills and the like is that such specifications should be reflected in the final test, after editing and pre-testing, in the proportions (with the weighting) that the specifications indicate as necessary. Traditional item analysis procedures and criteria for item rejection must therefore be applied with caution if the final test is to reflect the original specification.

One of the problems of the specification of microskills is that not all can be tested on any one text. This is revealing of the nature of such microskills: if they are not applicable to a particular text, to what extent are they generalisable skills? To what extent are they not rather **product**-oriented skills than **process**-oriented — in other words they are in effect glossable as 'the skill of processing X text feature' rather than '**how** X text feature is processed'. If X feature is not present in the text, the specific microskill as currently defined cannot be tested. If they were defined as process skills, then it might be possible to measure them, not on X feature, but on Y or Z features, which require a similar process. In fact, at present, the microskills are nothing more than the ability in general to process a certain linguistic feature.

Be that as it may, if one believes in the necessity for a specification of test content based on a needs analysis which will identify the types of skills that students do need, then it is crucial that test results should show how far individuals have met such specifications. One problem raised was: To what extent does the **lack** of such (pre-) specified skills lead to student problems or student failures? A further problem lies with the interpretation of the scores that result with a test specified in such a manner. Does any given score equal the same score gained by other testees? Are all 70%s to be interpreted in the same way? Surely, any less-than-perfect score will be composed of a different constellation of 'microskills'. Yet the claim that seems to be being made regarding microskills is that they are all equally necessary: no suggestion has been made that as long as one achieves, say 80% — **any** 80% — of the skills, one will no longer be 'at risk' linguistically. Presumably until further information is gathered about the relative importance of each microskill one will either have to regard perfection — 100% scores — as the only adequate test results, or, alternatively, be prepared to report 'scores' for each microskill — a sort of profile within a profile. It is true that the same predicament presents itself on a grammar test: any less-than-perfect score will comprise different successfully completed items. However, there is no claim associated with grammar tests that one **needs** mastery of modals, tenses, concord or whatever. How the score is arrived at is usually (although possibly erroneously) regarded as unimportant. The claims for enabling skills, microskills, are at present much stronger than that — possibly too strong, it was felt.

The question of specificity raised two further issues: that of extrapolation and that of comparability. Taking the latter first: how can one compare performances on two different, ie specific tests? If a medical student takes test A and an engineering student takes test B, how is one to determine whether a score of 50% on one test is equivalent to a score of 50% on the other? How are the parallel tests to be balanced and calibrated? Presumably one can only compare test performances if they are criterion-referenced: that is, scores are comparable when they all meet the criterion, or when they all fail to meet the criterion, since criterion-referenced scores are essentially binary. Thus, specific tests may well be necessarily criterion-referenced: the problem is, how to develop criterion-referenced tests. How does one establish the internal validity of such a test, and in particular how is one to conduct item analysis? (One answer suggested was point-biserial correlations). The problem of extrapolation, familiar from the discussion of performance tests, also exists with specific tests: How is one to predict from one performance on a specific test to performances in 'real-life'? Although the problem seems to be solved by needs analysis, which purportedly helps one to identify the real-life tasks and texts which one can incorporate in one's test, the fact is that increased specificity of the type brought about by needs analysis, particularly of a Munby nature, decreases the likelihood of extrapolability: the more specific the test/task, the less general can one be in one's conclusions from that text/task.

To what extent do proficiency tests have to be specific? Having seen the problems of specifying the level of specificity required, the discussion returned briefly, to the original question ('Who needs specific tests'?) to consider the extent to which any student coming to the UK to study can survive with only a limited range of skills, of the type identified by a needs analysis. Students themselves are reported as perceiving their greatest problems as being not related to Study Skills nor specific to their academic discipline, but rather to survival in British society: students consistently mention problems of adaptation to the UK, the problems of being immersed in a foreign environment. Frequent mention in the literature (see Davies, Moller & Adamson (1975), is made of the importance of social and welfare problems in the minds of overseas students: it is possible, however, that these 'welfare and social' problems might, to some extent at least, be linguistic or 'communicative' problems. Academic tutors may regard their students' subject knowledge (or lack of it), or their particular academic orientation, or their (non) adaptability as being their main problems. Yet these perceptions are often at odds with the students' own: are the tutors overlooking the real problems, or are the students unaware of their main difficulties, or reluctant to admit them?

What do Students Need?

The only way such questions can begin to be answered is through empirical study, both of the type carried out by Davies, Moller and Adamson (1975), and also by means of needs analysis. The aim of needs analysis is to answer the question: Proficiency for what? In this respect the *Specifications* document is valuable in pointing up the need to determine the communicative needs of students before establishing test content. Such needs analyses must be data-based: speculative research about the needs of 'typical' student is only of value if it susgests areas that empirical research might look at. One attempt to establish communicative needs is being made by Cyril Weir, with the Associated Examinations Board. Using an observation schedule adapted from Egglestone, Galton and Jones (1975) — the Science Teaching Observation Schedule — together with interviews with subject teachers, students, and follow-up questionnaires, Weir is attempting to do a needs analysis of interaction and events. His aim is to gain an overall impression of what happens in lectures, seminars and practical classes in Science, Engineering and Social Sciences courses with a view to finding activities and requirements which are common across disciplines, and which could therefore be incorporated in a test (which need not *a priori* be subject-specific). He aims to get a profile of types of activities, in order to see whether students can deal with the particular activities that the analysis shows they have to be able to deal with. It is hoped that a national questionnaire sent to staff and students in relevant departments will provide a broader basis for a description of what students have to do through language in respect of their courses and throw light on the language problems that staff and students have noticed. Although this is an interesting attempt to provide empirical justification for Study Skills tests or even subject-specific tests, there is a danger that mere observation will lead to a confusion of frequency of occurence with importance of an activity: 'the more frequent, the more important'. In fact, this is not necessarily the case: students may find relatively infrequent activities very difficult, and of crucial importance. The problem is to identify common areas of difficulty which are of importance. The hope, of course, is that if the test is built on a specification of what the student has to do, the receiving institution can judge whether a failure to do it is important for their particular course or for that particular student.

Another, practical problem of such research, apparent in Carroll's use of 'typical' data rather than real data, is the problem of sampling. Attempts to make general statements about what students need language for, inevitably come up against the sheer size of the research needed in order to be anything like exhaustive. Even a case study of one department in one university (see Murphy and Candlin, 1979), can take years of research without leading to generalisable results. Allied to such a practical problem is the problem posed by the need to specify, at least according to Munby/Carroll, the target levels and the tolerance conditions of language use. The whole area of tolerance conditions is very under-researched, and will require a vast amount of research effort before anything meaningful could begin to be said about the way in which native speakers judge foreigners' English: Are they more affected by occasional grammatical errors than by consistently poor handwriting or pro-nunciation? Does this vary from event to event (being different in seminars and tutorials, for example)? Including such parameters in our language tests is at best an ambitious goal, at worst impossible.

Profiles

The claim of *Specifications* and the justification for the existence of student 'profiles' is the 'fact' that a medical student needs x score on test A, y score on B and z score on test C, whereas an engineering student, for example, may require z score on test A, x score on test B and y score on text C. It was pointed out that we have no empirical evidence that such is the case (and we have suggested that it might equally plausibly be the case that a medical student simply needs a higher (lower) score overall on a particular test, than an engineering student). The point about profiles is that one needs different tests in order to produce them, and one needs to be able to show that such differentiated tests are necessary.

The aim of ELTS tests is to produce profiles, based upon the specifications arrived at by needs analysis. Information from an ELTS-type test might be of value diagnostically to teachers and syllabus designers. More traditional proficiency tests like EPTB and ELBA are not intended to yield diagnostic information, and although they are unfortunately frequently used as place-ment tests, they usually result in heterogeneous groups, in remedial or pre-sessional language courses for example. it could be that an ELTS-type test could be of use in identifying areas of students' weaknesses relative to their

131

communicative needs which would enable one to group together those students with a common problem and a common need to overcome it. This might suggest that whatever the problems involved in using an ELTS-type test for proficiency purposes, the diagnostic value of student profiles might be great. Proficiency tests cannot be used diagnostically, as they are designed simply to establish a criterion for a particular population in the most efficient way possible, whereas diagnostic tests, intended to yield richer information, could actually be used (though less efficiently) as proficiency tests. The question was raised as to why there are so few diagnostic tests in existence: is this merely a practical problem, or are diagnostic tests theoretically impossible? Or do they simply not exist because people — teachers — do not want them and would not use them? Even if it is possible to gather relevant diagnostic information, what could one do with the information? Students' problems may well depend on something not related to the point being tested, but on the content of the text, and a host of variables within the specific context of the problem. A diagnostic test will not in any case tell one which of the weaknesses identified are crucial weaknesses, since all it can do is establish whether a subject knows or does not know something about a particular area (although in a sense the importance of a weakness has been decided in advance by the very inclusion of items in that area, in the test). The view was put forward that diagnostic testing may be at best pretentious — making claims that it is unlikely to be able to live up to — or at worst a pseudo-procedure, because diagnosis is impossible: problems are not predictable. Of course, textbooks and syllabuses are just as pretentious to the extent that they attempt to eradicate or anticipate problems.

It was felt, however, that there may be a danger of requiring too much of our diagnostic profiles: we may not be able to achieve perfect diagnosis, but gross diagnoses may be of use. The information that a particular student cannot understand lectures but needs to, may well be of greater value than information to the effect that the same person has achieved a score of 32 on EPTB. Desirably, our diagnoses would yield information not only on the product — for example, for comprehension, 'this student has failed to understand this lecture' — but more valuably, would yield information on the process whereby the product was (not) reached. Product items cannot be used diagnostically, since they do not tell one anything about how the individual did or did not get the product, whereas process items might be of great value. Thus profiles might be of value if they are the right sort of profile: composed of 'items' that give information about process which is relevant to pedagogic intervention. This would seem to be less related to the question of the specificity of a language test, than to the question of test content in terms, for example, of enabling skills.

One real and important problem with profiles is that people — admissions officers and the like — do not seem to be able to cope with them. It was reported that there is a regrettable tendency to reduce ELTS-produced profiles to an 'average score', from which, of course, all diagnostic information has been removed. However desirable diagnostic profiles might be for some language teachers, it is unlikely that they will be usable by lay people. If tutors or admissions officers have difficulty understanding a division of scores into Listening and Reading, how likely are they to want, or to have the time, to interpret a profile? But even if such people have the time and the inclination to interpret profiles, to what extent will they be able to do so? There would have to be some sort of prior determination that x course in y department in z institution requires a certain sort of profile, and the fact is that we simply do not have that sort of information: neither the admissions officer nor the applied linguist is able to say what profile is required by any department in any institution. Thus, at best, a vast amount of research is necessary before such criteria could be established.

Research Needed

As was reiterated throughout this discussion, there is clearly a need for a great deal of research in the general area of specific purpose language proficiency testing before one can begin to make claims about the validity of particular approaches or tests. It would be unfortunate if ELTS-type tests were introduced without any sort of validation. Empirical evidence, rather than construct validity, is urgently required on these and similar tests, since already admissions decisions have been taken about students. It is to be hoped that follow-ups will be done of students who have been admitted with ELTS scores (although it is unlikely to be possible to follow-up students who have been rejected because of their ELTS scores). It would, for example, be perfectly possible to get ELTS-type profiles of students who emerge successfully from their course of study, and, over a period of time, to gather information which would lead to a profile of 'successful' students. The ethical problem of admitting or rejecting students without such information remains.

It was generally agreed that it is crucially important to find out what is happening on a test as influential as the ELTS test. There is a clear need to know how such 'ESP' tests relate to existing tests, for practical as well as academic reasons. There is a clear need to know what the new tests are predicting, and what they are capable of predicting. There is a need to know what sort of diagnostic information can validly be provided, and whether it can be used by both applied linguists and lay people. There is a need to specify much closer the outcomes to which the test is to relate: both the academic and the linguistic/communicative. There is a need to analyse the communicative needs of students in this country, and the extent to which the problems of native speakers are similar to or different from those of non-native speakers. It is clear that the design and implementation of a new test instrument requires an enormous amount of research, development, effort and resources, which it is easy to underestimate. The same need for research would exist for any test, but particularly for a test that appears to be an ESP test, that claims to be innovative, to be an improvement over other tests and that deals with the future of people. We need to know whether the claims made in the *Specifications* document are substantiated by the evidence. Nevertheless, it was agreed that the *Specifications* document is important, despite its unsubstantiated claims because it highlights the central problem of ESP proficiency testing: matching the demands of test design with those of the people taking the test and with those of the sponsoring and receiving institutions.

SECTION 3

BASIC CONCERNS IN TEST VALIDATION[1]

Adrian S Palmer, English Language Institute, University of Utah, USA
and Lyle F Bachman, University of Illinois, USA

Introduction

Test validity is a complex issue, and to address its many facets in any degree
of detail in the space available is a considerable challenge.[2] To make this
possible at all, we have had to assume that the reader has some degree of
familiarity with traditional views of validity. Consequently, we will review
only briefly the basic types of validity. We then look in somewhat more detail
into the nature of construct validity — the type of validity which we are
currently investigating. Finally, we present some of the general results we
have obtained in a recently completed construct validation study.

Types of Validity

Investigations of test validity are, in general, investigations into the extent to
which a test measures what it is supposed to measure. This is however, a very
general definition of validity, and it is useful to distinguish among several
different types of validity. We will distinguish among four here.

Face validity

The first, and in our opinion the least important, type of validity is 'face
validity'. Face validity is the appearance of validity — the extent to which a
test looks like it measures what it is supposed to, but without any empirical
evidence that it does. There is no statistical measure of face validity, and
there is no generally accepted procedure for determining that a test does or
does not demonstrate face validity.

---

[1] Prepared for presentation at the RELC Regional Seminar on the Evaluation and
Measurement of Language Competence and Performance, Singapore, April 21-25, 1980.

[2] We would like to express our deepest appreciation to the participants in the 1979 and
1980 colloquia on the construct validation of oral tests, held at the TESOL national
conventions. These individuals, too numerous to name here, have contributed to every
phase of the research described in this paper — from the original expression of a need
for such research to its design, implementation, and interpretaiton.

evidence that it does. There is no statistical measure of face validity, and there is no generally accepted procedure for determining that a test does or does not demonstrate face validity.

Content validity

The second, and a much more important, type of validity is 'content validity'. Content validity is the extent to which the selection of tasks one observes in a test-taking situation is representative of the larger set (universe) of tasks of which the test is assumed to be a sample. For example, if a test is designed to measure ability to speak a foreign language, yet requires the testee only to answer yes/no questions, one might doubt that this single task is representative of the sorts of tasks required in general conversation, which entails operations like greeting, leave-taking, questioning, explaining, describing, etc. The process of investigating content validity is basically a sampling process and requires a fairly complete description of the type of competence being tested.

Criterion-referenced validity

Another important but controversial type of validation is 'criterion-referenced validity'. Criterion-referenced validity is the extent to which a test predicts something that is considered important. For example, a test might predict success on a job, and, therefore, be very useful to an employer screening prospective employees.

It is important to note that in criterion-referenced validity, knowing exactly what a test measures is not crucial, so long as whatever is measured is a good predictor of the criterion behaviour. For example, a score on a translation test from a student's native language into English might be a very good predictor of how well a student would do in courses in an English-medium university — even though it might not be at all clear exactly what the translation test measures: the student's knowledge of English, his sensitivity to his native language, his ability to translate, his perseverance, or some combination of these or other abilities. One problem with criterion-referenced validity, then, is that a test can exhibit criterion-referenced validity without one's knowing what it measures.

Construct validity

The fourth type of validity is the relationship between a test and the psychological abilities it measures. This characteristic is called construct validity — the extent to which a test, or a set of tests, yield scores which behave in the ways one would predict they should if the researcher's theory of what is in the mind of the subject is correct. For example, if it is claimed that a test measures 'knowledge of grammar', one should be able to demonstrate that one can measure knowledge of grammar (as a psychological property) to a certain extent independently of other purported psychological properties such as 'knowledge of vocabulary', 'knowledge of the writing system', 'ability to reason verbally', etc.

Construct validation in the language testing field, then, is a process of hypothesis formation and hypothesis testing that allows the investigator to slowly zero in on the nature of the competence of the language user. As more and more construct validation studies are completed, researchers can say with more and more conviction that the evidence tends to support one position, and not another one.

The MT-MM C-D Construct Validation Procedure

One powerful procedure for investigating construct validity is called by the rather forbidding name 'multitrait-multimethod convergent-discriminant construct validation.' First described by Campbell and Fiske (1959), this procedure requires gathering data that will let one assess two types of validity: convergent and discriminant.

Convergent validity

Convergent validity is evidence that if one wants to measure something or other (a specific trait), one can measure it in a number of different ways (that is, by using different methods of measurement) and still come up with more or less the same results. In other words, it is an indication of how well test scores **agree.**

Discriminant validity

Discriminant validity, on the other hand, is an indication of the extent to which test scores **differ.** Here, one looks for evidence that tests which are supposed to measure different abilities (referred to as 'traits' or 'constructs') actually do provide different information. For example, if a test of the trait 'mathematical ability' and another of the trait 'verbal ability' always gave the same results, that is, if they ordered the subjects taking the tests in exactly the same ways, there would be no evidence that the mathematical and verbal ability traits were actually distinct. Now, in order to assess discriminant validity, it is necessary that one measure several traits at one time. This necessity is the source of 'multitrait' element in the name of the construct validation procedure.

137

The effect of method

The multitrait-multimethod research model assumes that test scores reflect not only what it is that one is attempting to measure (the trait), but also the effect of the methods of measurement. In other words, a test consists of both trait **and** method components.

To enable one to assess the relative contribution of trait and method to test scores, two or more traits must be measured by a minimum of two distinct methods. This stipulation is the source of the 'multimethod' element in the name of the procedure.

Types of Construct Validation Studies

Because of their complexity, a relatively small number of construct validation studies of language tests have been carried out. Those that have been are basically of three types: principal-component analytic studies; correlational studies; and confirmatory factor analytic studies.

Principal-component analytic studies

Principal-component analytic studies constitute the majority of the construct validation studies to date. Principal component analysis is a technique for accounting for as much common variance as possible on a set of different tests using a minimum number of factors. As it has been used, this analytic technique has been widely criticised. A comprehensive review of the criticisms would go far beyond the limited scope of this paper, and, in any case, such reviews are available in Thorndike (1971), Vollmer and Sang (1980), and Werts, Linn, and Joreskog (1971).

One general problem is that principal component analysis cannot be used to examine any kind of structural model in which the elements in the model are correlated (as appears to be the case in models of language proficiency). The reason for this is that principal component analysis looks only at variance structure, not covariance structure. (The structure model which we will present later will specify the magnitude of the correlation between the elements in the model.)

Another general problem is that of commonalities — this is, the amount of variance the analysis attributes to something the various measures have in common. The reason this is a problem is that the common variance in a principal component analysis contains measurement error and method variance, which inflate the magnitude of the common variance.

In short, principal component analysis not only does not allow only to test the likelihood of specific structural models, but it also produces results which may be inherently biased toward finding a large general factor, no matter what data is analysed.

John Oller has summarised the evidence from many of the principal component construct validation studies in the appendix to his new book, *Language Tests at School* (1979). Oller considers the results of the studies in terms of three hypotheses. The first is the divisibility hypothesis, according to which language proficiency is divisible into a number of distinct components, such as knowledge of grammar, knowledge of vocabulary, speaking ability, reading ability, and so on. The second hypothesis is the unitary competence hypothesis, according to which language proficiency **cannot** be broken down into a number of sub-components which can be differentially measured. This hypothesis predicts, for example, that reading knowledge and speaking knowledge (as measured by tests of each) cannot, in fact, be distinguished. A third hypothesis expresses a position somewhere between the first two. Called 'the partial divisibility hypothesis'; it posits that a major portion of test variance is unique to specific tests. Oller concludes, after considering the data from a number of studies, that the second hypothesis, the unitary competence hypothesis, seems to be a better explanation of the data.

Multitrait-multimethod correlational studies of language tests

Three construct validation studies using the multitrait-multimethod convergent-discriminant design referred to previously have been conducted: Brutsch (1979), Clifford (1978), and Corrigan and Upshur (1978). These studies have attempted to assess the construct validity of tests of purportedly different language use skills (such as reading and writing, and speaking) and purportedly different aspects of language (grammar, vocabulary, etc).

The primary (but not the only) analytic technique used is the examination of the pattern of intercorrelations of test scores according to criteria set forth by Campbell and Fiske (1959). These Campbell-Fiske criteria will be stated and applied, for illustrative purposes, to data from the Bachman-Palmer study described later in this paper.

The results of the three studies cited above are, in general, inconclusive. We believe these inconclusive results to be due, in part, to problems with the tests (such as low reliabilities) and in part to limitations of the analytic techniques used to evaluate the data. For example, an examination of the intercorrelation of test scores through the Campbell-Fiske framework does not even allow us to postulate an underlying causal model, much less to examine the plausibility of the three models hypothesised by Oller.

Multitrait-multimethod confirmatory factor analytic studies

Multitrait-multimethod confirmatory factor analytic studies employ experimental designs which allow the separation of the effects of traits and method on test scores. In addition, they employ an analytic statistical technique, called confirmatory factor analysis. Described in detail by Joreskog (1969), confirmatory factory analysis allows one to make a statistical comparison between structural predictions of a model and the results obtained in an empirical study. For example, given two alternative models of language proficiency, such as the unitary competence model and a two-factor divisible competence model, and given a sufficiently rich set of data (specifically, an over-identified model as described in Alwin (1974), the researcher can compare the explanatory power of the two models by applying statistical tests of goodness of fit of each model to the data.

The Bachman-Palmer Study

Origins of the study

Now we would like to describe a construct validation study whose origins go back to the summer of 1978. During the Fifth Congress of the International Association of Applied Linguistics at Montreal, Peter Groot suggested that despite the general interest in oral testing, attempts to assess the construct validity of oral tests were few. As a result of this conversation, Groot and Adrian Palmer contacted a group of researchers in language testing and arranged a two-day colloquium on the construct validation of oral tests at the 1979 TESOL convention in Boston. At this colloquium, the participants discussed the current state of affairs in the validation of oral tests. The general feeling of the participants was that the construct 'communicative competence in speaking' had not been adequately defined and that the convergent and discriminant validity of tests purporting to measure communicative competence in speaking had not been established. As a consequence, the participants recommended that a construct validation project be instigated.

The authors of this paper (Lyle F. Bachman and Adrian S Palmer) agreed to carry out this study with the advice of the members of the colloquium. In this study, we investigated the hypothesis that two language use skills, speaking and reading, which differ both in direction (productive versus receptive) and in channel (aural versus visual) are psychologically distinct and can be measured independently.

Design

In the study, we used three different methods of testing (namely, interview, translation, and self ratings) to investigate two hypothesised traits (namely, 'communicative competence in speaking' and 'communicative competence in reading'). To test two traits by means of three methods requires a minimum of six tests. The tests we used are described briefly in Figure 1. The tests are described in the boxes, with the names of the traits listed down the left column and the names of the methods listed across the top.

We administered all six tests to a population of 75 speakers of English as a second language at the University of Illinois at Urbana. All were native speakers of Mandarin Chinese. The subjects included students at the University and their spouses. All six tests were administered individually, and total testing time for each subject was approximately two hours.

Results of correlational analysis

The intercorrelations of scores on tests used in this study are presented in Table 1. Of the six tests administered, four (the interview tests of speaking and reading and the translation tests of speaking and reading) were rated by two different examiners. For the purpose of our analysis, we have considered each examiner's ratings as a separate method (or a separate test). Thus, Int-1 on Table 1 stands for the interview as rated by interviewer number 1. Int-2 stands for the interview as rated by interviewer number 2, and so on. Considering the data in this way allowed us to set up a 10 x 10 matrix of inter-correlations.

Convergent validity

The first hypothesis tested concerns convergent validity. The hypothesis states that correlations between scores on tests of the same trait which employ different methods (called validity indices) should be significant and positive. These validity indices are enclosed in the upper left and lower right triangles. All of these correlations are significant and positive, thus providing evidence of convergent validity for both the speaking and the reading tests.

Discriminant validity

The next two hypotheses tested concern discriminant validity. The first hypothesis is that correlations between different tests of the same trait (validity indices) should be higher than correlations between tests having neither trait nor method in common.

141

An example will illustrate exactly how this hypothesis is tested. Consider the validity indices in the left column of the upper left triangle (.88, .77, .76, and .51). These are correlations between test #1 (examiner #1's ratings on the oral interview test) with the scores on all other tests of speaking. We now wish to compare these with correlations between tests which share neither trait nor method. This set of correlations includes all the indices in the first column of the lower left hand box **except** the index inside the diagonal (.54).

For example, let us compare the .88 validity index with the four relevant indices in the column below it (.56, .58, .52, and .44). .88 is higher than all of these indices — providing evidence of discriminant validity. Note, however, that one of the validity indices in column 1 (.51) is lower than some of the indices in the column below it. If we work through all possible comparisons, we find that the first discriminant validity hypothesis is confirmed in 28 out of 40 cases for speaking, and 38 out of 40 cases for reading.

The second discriminant validity hypothesis is that correlations between tests of the same trait (the validity indices) should be higher than correlations between tests of **different** traits measured by the **same** method. Evidence for this type of validity is harder to obtain, since one has to find **low** correlations between tests which share the **same** method of testing. If the effect of the method is strong, it can exert a strong effect on pairs of test scores which share method.

To test this hypothesis, one compares the same set of validity indices used to test the previous hypothesis with the index within the diagonal in the lower left hand box. This criterion for discriminant validity is clearly met when we compare validity index .88 with the .54 index below it. It is clearly not met, however, when we compare the validity index .51 with the .54 index below it. Again, if one works through all possible comparisons, one finds that the second discriminant validity hypothesis is confirmed in 7 out of 10 cases for speaking and 4 out of 10 cases for reading.

The effect of method is particularly noticeable in tests using translation or self-rating methods. Of the indices in the diagonal in the lower left hand box, the intercorrelations between tests 3-5 which employ translation and self-rating methods (.64, .69, and .68) are clearly higher than those between tests 1 and 2 which do not (.54 and .46).

This completes an examination of the correlations using Campbell-Fiske criteria. We would like to emphasise once again that there are a number of problems associated with the Campbell-Fiske criteria (see Althauser, 1974) which lead us to favour confirmatory factor analysis, the results of which we turn to now.

Confirmatory factor analysis

Confirmatory factor analysis, as we have noted before, is a technique for statistically evaluating the goodness of fit of competitive causal models to a body of data. We have tested over ten models against our data, each involving different assumptions about trait-method interaction. The models with the best fit assume **no** trait-by-method interaction. In keeping with the limited goals of this paper, we present the results of the analysis of only two models. One model posits three method factors and **one** posits three method factors and **two** trait factors: competence in speaking and in reading (a version of the divisible competence hypothesis). The results of the confirmatory factor analysis are given in Table 2.

To test the hypothesis of distinct speaking and reading traits, we examined the difference between the chi squares of the unitary language factor model (50.722) and of the two trait model (34.980). The difference is significant at the $p. < 001$ level. Thus, we reject the hypothesis that a single language factor underlies the variables.

Having found that the model which best accounts for the data comprises two language traits (speaking and reading) and three methods (interview, translation, and self ratings), we examined the loading of each test on each of these five factors (as well as a uniqueness factor which includes specificity and measurement error components). Factor loads of the ten tests of the six factors are given in Table 3.

The high loading of the oral interview measures on the speaking factor (.819), compared to the relatively lower loading of the oral translation measures (.568) and the oral self-rating measure (.298), indicates that the oral interview method provides a better measure of speaking ability than do the translation and self-rating methods. An examination of the loadings of the interview, translation and self-rating measure on the reading factor leads us, by similar reasoning, to conclude that the translation measure (with a loading of .756 on the reading factor) provides the best measure of reading ability.

Loadings of the measures on the three methods factors (interview, translation, and self-rating) support these conclusions. Specifically, the oral tests load less heavily on the interview method factor (.459) than they do on the translation method factor (.729) and on the self-rating method factor (.734). This indicates that the effect of the method of testing on oral test scores is **least** for the interview method. In other words, assuming we are interested in maximising the effect of the **trait** (which we are trying to measure) and minimising the effect of **method** (which we are not trying to measure), we would choose the interview method to measure oral ability.

Looking at the effect of method on the reading test scores, we find that the translation method (which loads .611 on the reading tests) affects the reading test scores less than the self-rating method (.834) or the interview method (.972). We conclude, therefore, that of the three methods used in the study, the one which minimises the effect of test method on the reading test scores is the translation method.

The results of the confirmatory factor analysis can be presented in the form of a path diagram for the multitrait-multimethod model comprising two traits and three methods. This diagram is given in Figure 2. M_{1-3} and T_{1-2} are the three method and two trait factors which, confirmatory factor analysis indicates, best account for the scores on the measures (the X's). Double ended arrows indicate correlations. Single-ended arrows indicate factor loadings. Single-ended arrows from a number to a measure indicate the loading of that measure on a uniqueness factor — a factor which includes measure specific non-random variance as well as random error variance.

Summary

We feel that this study, and the two years of planning and discussion that preceded it, have yielded two important results: one methodological, the other empirical.

With respect to methodology, we feel that the application of confirmatory factor analysis to a body of data gathered in such a manner as to make it possible to identify and quantify the effects of trait and method on test scores allow us a far clearer picture of the nature of measured language proficiency than has been available using other types of analysis.

With respect to our empirical findings, we feel we have found strong evidence supporting Oller's divisible language competence model. In addition, we have evidence that of the three methods we used to evaluate proficiency in speaking and reading, the interview method provided the best measure of speaking and the translation method the best measure of reading. This should somewhat reassure the United States Foreign Service Institute, which has, up to now, had to rely primarily on faith and on face validity to justify their using these two methods in their testing programme.

Having obtained evidence for the distinctness of the speaking and reading traits, we are now in a position to examine further (1) the extent to which a common factor may or may not underly these distinct traits or (2) the composition of the individual traits.

Table 1
MTMM Correlation Matrix
All correlations sig at p < . 01, df = 74

Speaking (A)

		Int-1 (1)	Int-2 (2)	Trans-1 (3)	Trans-2 (4)	Self (5)
A	1	1.00				
	2	.88	1.00			
	3	.77	.72	1.00		
	4	.76	.72	.85	1.00	
	5	.51	.56	.46	.53	1.00
B	1	.54	.45	.62	.65	.58
	2	.56	.46	.64	.67	.60
	3	.58	.61	.64	.68	.46
	4	.52	.55	.62	.69	.49
	5	.44	.45	.47	.51	.68

Reading (B)

		Int-1 (1)	Int-2 (2)	Trans-1 (3)	Trans-2 (4)	Self (5)
B	1	1.00				
	2	.97	1.00			
	3	.65	.65	1.00		
	4	.65	.65	.94	1.00	
	5	.68	.68	.54	.54	1.00

Table 2
Comparison of chi squares for two models

Rater factor
loadings equal

	Model 1
1 Trait	$\chi^2 = 50.722$ $df = 30$ $p = .0104$
	Model 2
2 Traits	$\chi^2 = 34.980$ $df = 29$ $p = .2052$ $r\lambda_{ti}\lambda_{tj} = .524$
difference	$\chi_1^2 - \chi_2^2 = 15.742$ $df = 1$ $p < .001$

Figure 1
Multitrait-multimethod matrix for the Bachman-Palmer construct validation study

Methods / Traits	Interview (1)	Translation (2)	Self-ratings (3)
Communicative competence in speaking (A)	For. Serv. Inst. (FSI) interview test of speaking	Translation test of speaking. Direct translation of dialogue from subject's native language into spoken English.	Self-ratings of speaking ability
Communicative competence in reading (B)	Interview test of reading. Subject is interviewed in his native language about contents of English reading passages.	Translation test of reading. Direct translation from English reading passages to subject's native language.	Self-ratings of reading ability

Table 3

Factor loadings (and standard errors) for measures

Measures	Speaking	Reading	Interview	Translation	Self-Rating	Uniqueness
Oral Interview 1	.819 (.082)	.000	.459 (.126)	.000	.000	.113
Oral Interview 2	.819 (.082)	.000	.459 (.126)	.000	.000	.132
Oral Translation 1	.568 (.091)	.000	.000	.729 (.098)	.000	.175
Oral Translation 2	.568 (.091)	.000	.000	.729 (.098)	.000	.137
Oral Self-rating	.298 (.097)	.000	.000	.000	.734 (.108)	.357
Reading Interview 1	.000	.155 (.140)	.972 (.085)	.000	.000	.034
Reading Interview 2	.000	.155 (.140)	.972 (.085)	.000	.000	.017
Reading Translation 1	.000	.756 (.097)	.000	.611 (.133)	.000	.044
Reading Translation 2	.000	.756 (.097)	.000	.611 (.133)	.000	.070
Reading Self-rating	.000	.216 (.113)	.000	.000	.834 (.104)	.235

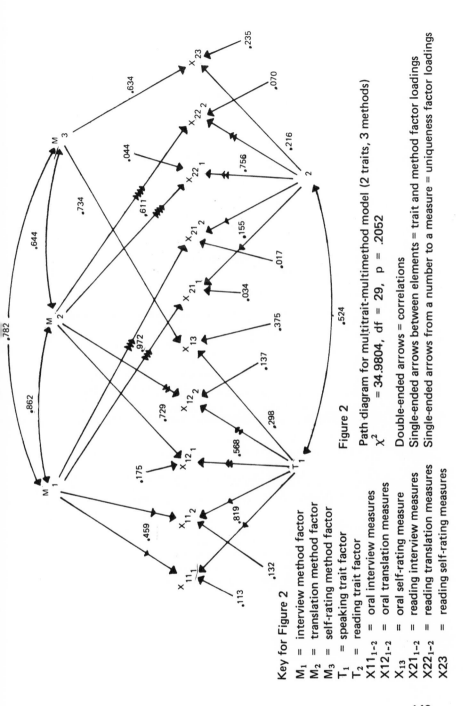

Key for Figure 2

M₁ = interview method factor
M₂ = translation method factor
M₃ = self-rating method factor
T₁ = speaking trait factor
T₂ = reading trait factor
X11₁₋₂ = oral interview measures
X12₁₋₂ = oral translation measures
X13 = oral self-rating measure
X21₁₋₂ = reading interview measures
X22₁₋₂ = reading translation measures
X23 = reading self-rating measures

Figure 2

Path diagram for multitrait-multimethod model (2 traits, 3 methods)
χ^2 = 34.9804, df = 29, p = .2052

Double-ended arrows = correlations
Single-ended arrows between elements = trait and method factor loadings
Single-ended arrows from a number to a measure = uniqueness factor loadings

149

BIBLIOGRAPHY

ALHAUSER, ROBERT P
Inferring validity from the multitrait-multimethod matrix: another assessment. In: CONSTNER, H L, *ed.* Sociological Methodology 1973-1974.

ALWIN, DUNNE F
Approaches to the interpretation of relationships in the multitrait-multimethod matrix. In: COSTNER, H L, *ed.* Sociological Methodology 1973-1974. San Francisco: Jossey-Bass, 1974.

BRUTSCH, SUSANNA M
Convergent/discriminant validation of prospective teacher proficiency in oral and written production of French by means of the MLA Cooperation Foreign Language Proficiency Tests. French Direct Proficiency Tests for Teachers (TOP and TWT) and self-ratings. PhD Dissertation. University of Minnesota, Minneapolis, Minnesota, 1979.

CAMPBELL, D T and FISKE, D W
Convergent and discriminant validation by the multitrait-multimethod matrix. In: Psychological Bulletin, *56*, 2, 1959.

CLIFFORD, REV T
Reliability and validity of language aspects contributing to oral proficiency of prospective teachers of German. In: CLARK, John L D, *ed.* Direct testing of speaking proficiency: theory and application. Princeton, New Jersey: Educational Testing Service, 1978.

CORRIGAN, ANNE and UPSHUR, JOHN A
Test method and linguistic factors in foreign language tests. (Paper presented at the 1978 TESOL Convention, Mexico City)

JORESKOG, K G
A general approach to confirmatory maximum likelihood factor analysis. In: Psychometrika, *34*, 183-202, 1969.

OLLER, JOHN W, Jr.
Language tests at school. London: Longman, 1979.

THORNDIKE, ROBERT L
Educational measurement. 2nd ed (Chapters 14 and 16). American Council on Education, 1971.

VOLLMER, HELMUT J, and SANG, F
On the psycholinguistic construct of an internalised expectancy grammer.
(Paper presented at the 2nd Colloquium on the Construct Validation of
Oral Tests, 1980 TESOL National Convention, San Francisco, California,
4-5 March, 1980)

WERTS, C E, LINN, R L, and JORESKOG, K G
Estimating the parameters of path models involving unmeasured variables.
In BLALOCK, H M, Jr, *ed.* Causal models in the social sciences. Chicago:
Aldine-Atherton, 1971.

WHY ARE WE INTERESTED IN GENERAL LANGUAGE PROFICIENCY?[1]

Helmut J Vollmer, University of Osnabrück, Germany

Introduction

I should like to start out by saying that language proficiency is what language proficiency tests measure. This circular statement is about all one can firmly say when asked to define the concept of proficiency to date. This is even more so when it comes to the construct of overall language proficiency, regardless of whether we want to refer to one's mother tongue or any second or foreign language. What exactly is this general language proficiency, does it really exist and what, then, is our particular interest in this construct either as test researchers, or as test developers or as users of test results? What models of general language proficiency (GLP) seem to be plausible, on what grounds and based on what theoretical insights? Is the concept of GLP related more to the competence level of a person, that is, to what the learner knows about a certain language (including knowledge about how to use it) or does it rather refer to the performance or skill level on which the learner actually demonstrates his/her knowledge in more or less meaningful communicative situations? If we consider proficiency to be a performance category we should then try and define it as some sort of attained level of mastery within a given language which can be observed and measured by a number of different methods. We would then immediately face the question in which way precisely GLP might differ from the sum or average of one's scores on any of the existing proficiency measures covering different aspects of language that one might be able to name (if not isolate). If we think, however, of GLP as an underlying ability to demonstrate one's knowledge of a language regardless of the nature of the task involved, the skill(s) implied, the measurement method used etc., we would then have to elaborate on the differences between the two terms 'overall proficiency' and 'competence' (if there are any at all) — no matter what theoretical framework for linguistic and/or communicative competence we may have in mind.

Question after question arises once we investigate more deeply into the concept of GLP which is not clear at all as yet. In my paper I would like to share with you some of the problems which my colleague Dr Sang and I came

---

[1] I would like to thank my friend and colleague Fritz Sang for his valuable comments on an earlier draft of this paper. Of course, I assume full responsibility for the views expressed here as well as for all kinds of errors.

across in studying the structure of what we thought to be 'linguistic competence' in German learners of English as a foreign language. The research project that I am referring to is based at the Max-Planck-Institut für Bildungsforschung in Berlin. One of the main objectives of this project is to study the theoretical claims and empirical evidence put forward in support of either the 'unitary competence' hypothesis or the 'divisible competence' hypothesis and to further contribute to this controversy by presenting our own research findings and careful interpretation of them (cf. Sang/Vollmer 1978). The basic question here is — as you might know - whether or not all performances in a second/foreign language can be traced back to a single underlying factor, the so-called 'General Language Proficiency Factor' (GLPF) and whether or not it seems theoretically plausible and valid to interpret the appearance of such a factor as an indication of the existence of a unitary cognitive ability at work. If so, the wide-spread belief in relatively distinguishable, more or less autonomous dimensions of linguistic competence and their realisation on the performance level (the 'four skills') which most foreign language teaching (and testing) nowadays is still based upon would have to be questioned, if not overthrown. The research situation concerning this problem, which implies one of the central issues of language testing theory, is quite controversial. Basically speaking there are two different lines of research which operate to some extent apart from one another (without really relating their arguments and tentative findings to each other). Let me now turn to a brief outline of these two positions with respect to their definition of proficiency in theoretical and operational terms.

Conflicting views of language proficiency

1 The divisible competence hypothesis

The first of the two research branches referred to has concentrated on attempting to identify those areas/dimensions of linguistic achievement which could be interpreted along the lines of meaningful learning objectives and which were able to structure the learning and teaching process of a second/ foreign language in a plausible way. Theoretically this approach is based on the more or less implicit assumption that there is (most likely) no such thing as a single unitary language ability but (more likely) a number of specific linguistic — and non-linguistic — competencies or areas of competence underlying language behaviour. It is hoped that these competencies can be identified and related to each other more distinctly and systematically as our knowledge advances, and that they can be further broken down some day into sub-competencies, eg into components or aspects contributing to the successful operation of a certain area of competence. It must be added, however, that within the last twenty years there has never been a strong version of this claim. Rather a great number of researchers seem to have adopted this general outlook (possibly for lack of a convincing theoretical alternative) and used a multidimensional 'model' as their unquestioned starting point. Accordingly, they have devoted time and effort only in identifying and naming those competencies that could be plausibly related to the different skills or aspects of language behaviour on the performance level. In addition, investigation into the structure of foreign language aptitude seemed to support the view that the acquisition of another language other than one's native tongue was dependent on at least three different language-specific factors within the learner (besides non-linguistic variables like motivation etc.).

This approach has been labelled (somewhat unjustly as I believe) the 'discrete-point approach', although in reality (at least for its most outspoken proponents) it has always been a mixture of 'discrete-point' tests and some 'global' testing (see, for example, the matrices given in Valette (1967) or Harris (1969); for a discussion of this 'disjunctive fallacy' as a whole cf Farhady (1979).

Certainly sets of items that test the control of specific elements of the second language (phonemes, intonation patterns, vocabulary or structural items, and the like) are discrete-point tests, as most multiple-choice items are discrete-point items. But the testing of the so-called 'integrated skills' like reading or listening with comprehension questions based on a longer reading or listening test do in my understanding very much focus on global aspects of the language independent of the item format used. Tasks like these require the integration of different elements of knowledge in order to understand and interpret language in context. Even if a longer reading or listening passage is scored on the basis of specific elements implied (in a manner that parallels discrete-point items) I would still consider it to be a global measure more than anything else. As concerns language proficiency it was normally thought of as being best approached by a whole battery of language tests (instead of only one or just a few). Each of the tests was supposed to aim at a unique aspect of knowing a language and/or handling it on different levels.

As early as 1961 J B Carroll worked out a rationale for describing and measuring language proficiency along the multidimensional lines outlined above. Carroll pointed out that the validity of a proficiency test does not only depend on whether a representative sample of the English language had been covered. It is more important yet, according to Carroll, that the success of the testee in coping with future language situations, future learning situations as well as certain forseeable social situations in real life can be adequately predicted with some degree of certainty on the basis of the test results. Therefore one has to select and combine those dimensions of test performance which are relevant to future tasks and situations. In other words, the proficiency of a learner (his degree of mastery of the foreign language) cannot be judged or measured in abstract terms. A test of proficiency, according to Carroll, has always to be validated externally against the criterion of 'having sufficient English to operate in given situations' (Carroll 1972:315). Carroll goes on to specify ten relevant dimensions of test performance which include those elementary aspects of knowledge and the four integrated skills: listening comprehension, reading comprehension, speaking and written composition. These dimensions are to be combined in a specific manner each time. They should be given different weighting according to their relative importance depending on the purpose of the testing and based on the findings of future job or task analysis, that is, on the results of the externally validated description of qualifications needed.

As far as I can see the term 'overall proficiency' or 'GLP' was never used (and maybe has no place) within this theoretical framework. As long as the purpose of proficiency testing is to determine whether a learner's language ability corresponds to specified language requirements it makes more sense to speak of a learner's 'specific proficiency' in relation to the content area defined and the criteria used. For example, in placement tests we want to know whether a student is proficient enough to enter this or that course, or we want to find out whether a learner is to able to read professional literature in another language with a specific level (such as 80 or 90 per cent) of accuracy, etc. The Foreign Service Institute of the United States has developed a number of proficiency tests that are meant to indicate to what degree a person can function in the foreign language. Again, the reported language ability of a candidate is defined by a predetermined set of functional categories: having sufficient German, Spanish, Russian etc. to carry out an informal conversation, to chair a meeting, to explain a statement of policy, to do this or that . . .

In all of these cases nobody would dare to make a judgement on a person's overall foreign language proficiency, but only on a limited, yet seemingly well-defined aspect of language proficiency based on the tests used. The crucial question, of course, is that of validity: do the tests really measure what they purport to measure, what language tasks, what content areas, what communicative situations etc. are being sampled, how are the levels of correctness and appropriateness being defined and identified, how justified are the predictions made as to a person's functioning in that language? The very problems of sampling and prediction suggest that we always include some judgement of a learner's 'transfer ability' (if he or she is able to act with language in this or that test situation, he or she will probably be similarly successful in situations not included in the test or not forseeable at all). In other words, a certain understanding of a person's generalised state of knowledge or ability to use this knowledge — however vague — seems to be implied in any proficiency concept. It is exactly here where the second of the two research branches starts.

2   The notion of 'overall proficiency'

In the late sixties it was Spolsky who asked: What does it mean to know a language or how do you get someone to perform his competence (as contradictory as this formulation sounds). He argues that 'knowledge of a language' was more than having command over a certain amount of vocabulary or mastering its isolated elements. It was **knowing the rules** of a language, as he put it.

> Knowing a language is a matter of having mastered these (as yet incompletely specified) rules; the ability to handle new sentences is evidence of knowing the rules that are needed to generate them (Spolsky 1973: 173).

Spolsky thus reminds us of 'two vital truths about language, the fact that language is redundant, and the fact that it is creative' (1973: 167). To him knowledge of a language, being a matter of knowledge of rules, is the same as 'underlying linguistic competence'. This operates in all the different kinds of performances, be they active or passive (the latter being an equally creative process on the part of the learner).

Almost everyone would agree with Spolsky so far. It is worth noting that he only speaks of an 'underlying linguistic competence', not of a 'unitary competence'. In another context he considers knowledge of rules to be the 'principal factor' (1973: 174) in the understanding as well as in the pro-duction of messages (not the one and only factor explaining all sorts of language behaviour). This distinction which I try to make here is quite important. It becomes clearer, I think, when we follow Spolsky's suggestion that we could find out about 'knowledge of a language' equally well when testing passive or active skills:

> This last does not of course mean that an individual's performance as a speaker is the same as his performance as a listener; such a claim would clearly be ridiculous, for it would be tantamount to saying that anyone who could read a Shakespeare play could also write it. All that it does claim is that the same linguistic competence, the same knowledge of rules, underlies both kinds of performance.
> (Spolsky 1973: 174).

I take this quotation to be a clear indication of the shift of focus from the differences between the skills (and how they might relate to underlying competencies) to what they might have in common by way of a shared basic competence stretching out into all the skills. But in trying to explain the ability to read (and understand!) a Shakespeare play or to write one we will have to take other competencies (constructs) into account — besides and on top of 'knowledge of rules'. If our focus of interest is concentrated on the assumed central linguistic competence (or that portion which may be common to the operation in all the skills) the additional cognitive forces (those which are **not** common to all the skills) do not disappear — they are simply out of focus (for the time being).

My interpretation of the concept of an 'underlying linguistic competence', which does not imply it to be necessarily unitary, is somewhat dimmed again by Spolsky's introduction of another term, that of 'overall proficiency' (1973: 175).

> some way to get beyond the limitation of testing a sample of surface features, and seek rather to tap underlying linguistic competence
> (Spolsky 1973: 175).

This sentence can easily be misunderstood in that it suggests that competence of a foreign language learner can be **tested directly** (or at least more directly) rather than measured through any of its manifestations of the performance level known so far — which is not possible! What Spolsky refers to is the development of 'competence-oriented' tests (others say 'integrative' tests) as valid indicators of learners' success in handling actual performance, calling for normal language functioning based on the principles of redundancy and creativity.

The sentence quoted above could very well nourish a second misunderstanding by suggesting that linguistic competence can be measured by a (singular!) test of overall proficiency. Moreover, the term 'overall' does not only imply 'basic', but also 'comprehensive', as if **all** the possible aspects of a person's language behaviour (and the ability structure governing his or her performance) could be grasped exhaustively in one proficiency measure. This view, though, is not shared by the author quoted. When asked at the 1974 Washington Language Testing Symposium for a clear definition of overall proficiency, Spolsky answered:

> It should be obvious by now that I can't say that precisely, or I would have. It's an idea that I'm still playing with. It has to correlate with the sum of various kinds of things in some way, because it should underlie

any specific abilities. In other words, I have the notion that ability to operate in a language includes a good, solid central portion (which I'll call overall proficiency) plus a number of specific areas based on experience and which will turn out to be either the skill or certain sociolinguistic situations

(Jones/Spolsky 1975: 69).

Taking this uncertainty as it is, other authors like John W Oller had picked up the notion of overall proficiency and had experimented in the meantime with a number of measures in foreign language testing aimed at tapping the postulated GLP, namely with different form of the Cloze test and dictation.

3   The unitary competence hypothesis

Oller and others believe that there are good reasons for assuming that linguistic competence is not only the principal factor underlying all language skills, but that this competence is unitary (cf for example Oller 1976, Oller/ Hinofotis 1976). In his theoretical work Oller tries to convince us that this (assumed) unitary competence is more than just a construct, that it 'really exists'. In addition, he asserts that all processes of comprehending and producing utterances, of understanding and conveying meaning (in whatever mode by whatever medium) are governed by this one indivisible intellectual force – in L1 as well as in any L2. In terms of psycholinguistic modelling Oller has offered an interpretation of this assumed force (or basic human ability) as an 'internalised expectancy grammar' at work (cf Oller 1974; 1978). This concept can be based partly on research done in cognitive psychology, especially as to perceptual processes in general (not restricted to language perception). On the other hand one has to be rather careful in adopting or applying results or non-language-specific insights from cognitive psychology to a theory of language processing. Neisser himself, one of the authorities in that field, turns out to be much more cautious in 1976 than in his basic work published in 1967 (for further discussion of the plausibility of Oller's psycholinguistic construct 'expectancy grammer' see Vollmer/Sang 1979).

As to the comparison of language reception and language production as psychological processes, their structural equation does not seem justified at the moment or it seems a bit overhasty at least. Though the results of psycholinguistic research to date indeed suggest some commonalities between the encoding and the decoding system, production and comprehension can probably not be seen as mirror images. Many attempts have been made to account for their unique characteristics by postulating different underlying processes. The role played by syntax is a case in point here. To our present knowledge, the syntactic level seems to be much more important for the process of planning and producing an utterance than for perceiving and decoding it, whereas in the latter case the semantic level seems to be predominant. Generally speaking, the differences between knowing how to analyse input and knowing how to construct output apparently outweigh the correspondences between these two processes. Evidence continues to come in from many sources that language as comprehension and language as production are so profoundly different that any attempt to describe language 'non-directionally', or neutrally with respect to its interpretive and expressive functions, will be highly controversial, if not fail. I am not ready, however, to claim that there are basically two distinguishable competences, one associated with understanding language, one with producing meaningful utterances (although this might be so). This 'two competences hypothesis' may be considered to replace the construct of one indivisible linguistic competence — or else all the competences named could be looked upon as hierarchically ordered, pertaining to different levels, each having its own scope, not excluding one another (theoretically). I know that a position like mine would need further explication to be better understood and needs, above all, further research to back it up and make it more plausible. Unfortunately, I cannot go into it any deeper in this paper (for discussion of some aspects, however, cf Fodor, Bever, Garrett 1974; Straight 1976; Vollmer/ Sang forthcoming).

My main point here is that almost anything one can say about language processing, especially about speech production, is still very speculative, even by the standards current in psycholinguistics. There are a vast number of uncertainties and many open research questions to be solved before any one of the theoretical models can hope to reflect psychological reality (a claim that Oller makes). One of the major problems with the writing of Oller, then, is the speediness with which (suitable) pieces of research from other disciplines are incorporated into his theoretical framework — and the firmness with which certain positions are taken forcing the reader to follow (and believe!) the expert — as if no doubt were possible. From a theoretical point of view the notion of a general language proficiency as the manifestation of an underlying unitary competence interpreted along the lines of an expectancy grammar is still very vague and not convincing at all (as we shall see in more detail in the next section). So is the empirical evidence for both the unitary and the divisible competence hypothesis (as I shall point out later).

General language proficiency defined

In this part of my paper I would like to develop some of the critical points concerning the notion of GLP and the testing of proficiency in a more systematic way. I have organised my thoughts under three different headings:

Proficiency and competence
General language proficiency and cognition
The dynamics of general language proficiency

1 Proficiency and competence

Let us reconsider once more whether proficiency, especially the concept of a GLP, pertains to the performance level and thus to overt language behaviour, or whether it represents a construct on the competence level reflecting our understanding of how we think that different uses of a language have been integrated internally within a learner. One dictionary which I looked up defines proficiency as an 'advanced state of attainment in some knowledge, art, or skill.' Such a definition is useful though it must be elaborated upon, especially since both the knowledge and the skill level could be meant if someone is said to be proficient.

When we turn to Carroll's (1968: 57) suggested chart of linguistic performance abilities (all based on assumed underlying competences) it becomes evident that according to this author the term 'proficiency' relates neither to actual (and measurable) performances not to the competence level in the sense of knowledge of a language. The 'proficiencies' or aspects of proficiency seem to form a level of their own — somewhere in between performance and competence (in the Chomskyan sense of the terms). Carroll (1968) speaks of linguistic performance abilities. Their relative degree of development decides what a person's language proficiency looks like, what it is made up of, which of his or her performance abilities contributes to what extent to the overall picture (expressed by a total score) of mastery of a second language. In discussing Carroll's earlier work on *Fundamental Considerations in Testing for English Language Proficiency of Foreign Students* (1972) I have already pointed out that in testing proficiency we are not only interested in an examinee's actual strengths or weaknesses, in particular fields of linguistic knowledge or lack of it. What we are mainly concerned about is how this knowledge is put to use, how bits and pieces of this knowledge are being integrated on different levels of performance, how language is handled with more or less facility in terms of the total communicative effect of an utterance. Another important aspect in this context is, of course, a person's ability to get by even in situations where knowledge is deficient, where uncertainties as to the appropriateness of an utterance according to social conventions exist or psychological restrictions in interaction have to be dealt with. To these latter aspects more attention has been paid ever since the broader concept of communicative competence (made up of linguistic competence plus something else which we have yet better to define) has been introduced (cf the recent work of Canale/Swain 1979, especially their concept of strategic competence which comprises something equivalent to Carroll's linguistic performance abilities plus a set of less language-bound social-interactional abilities).[2]

Carroll's view of foreign language proficiency focusing on the narrower construct of linguistic competence can probably best be summarised as an accumulated index of a person's (predictable) mastery of and functioning in L2. This index is inferred from actual measurements on different levels of performance, which are taken to be manifestations of covert linguistic performance abilities which in turn are all thought to be based on underlying competences.

Let us find out now how the notion of GLP relates to the performance and competence level. It was Spolsky in 1975 who stated clearly that overall proficiency could not be considered identical with linguistic competence.

> It's something that presumably has what Alan Davies would call construct validity. In other words, it depends on a theoretical notion of knowledge of a language and the assumption that while this knowledge at a certain level can be divided up into various kinds of skills, there is something underlying the various skills which is obviously not the same as competence. You have to allow, of course, for gross differences. For example, if somebody is deaf he won't be good at reading or writing, and if somebody has never been exposed to speech of a certain variety he won't be good at handling that. And after allowing for those gross, very specific differences of experience, whatever is left is overall proficiency
> (Jones/Spolsky 1975: 67).

---

[2] Canale/Swain (1979) postulate three different dimensions of communicative competence in their theoretical framework: grammatical competence, sociolinguistic competence, and strategic competence. After having reviewed all the relevant literature it appears very unlikely to these authors that communicative competence could be reduced to only one global language proficiency dimension.

The model of Canale/Swain, however, is not yet based on any empirical investigation, as far as I know.

Apparently the basic idea is that a speaker of a second language acquires not only certain skills but at the same time builds up a general understanding of that language (knowledge of the rules). In other words, it is suggested that all speakers develop and have a general proficiency simply by being exposed to a language. This GLP may be acquired by different sense modalities, but once it is there it can then be employed in any of the skill areas — even in those not particularly trained. It can also be applied to a vast number of future situations - even to those which are not foreseeable. 'Theoretically, at least, two people could know very different parts of a language and, having a fairly small part in common, still know how to get by. That's where overall proficiency becomes important' (Jones/Spolsky 1975: 69). It almost looks as if GLP stays with a person once it has been formed. On the other hand it seems to be a cognitive potential consisting of language-specific knowledge (sets of rule systems) being stored which is thought to be the software of a generalised ability to operate in that language. Spolsky gives the following (construed) example:

> Someone is exposed to the traditional method of learning a language, that is, a grammar-translation approach at school, and then goes to live in the country for two months. At the beginning of the two months that person would test out completely at O or something on any kind of oral test. But he already has this overall proficiency that is just waiting for new experiences
>
> (Jones/Spolsky 1975: 70).

Although many questions remain unanswered it should be pointed out in summarising that for researchers like Spolsky and even more so for Oller the notion of GLP has become a psychological construct, something non-observable any more. It has thus moved in its theoretical meaning towards the competence level, with a clear connotation of an unfolding cognitive ability to operate in a language.

2 General language proficiency and cognition

In my opinion when we are chasing after GLP what we really want to get at is the centre of what might be called the **general cognitive apparatus** of a person. Whether theoretically justified or not we hope to be able to form a quick and somewhat overall picture of a learner's generalised ability to make use of the instrument of a foreign language more or less successfully in all possible situations. We are not concerned about the previous training of a testee or any curriculum programme in particular (in this respect proficiency tests differ from achievement testing). On the contrary we are looking for a more or less sound basis in order to make predictions about a person's future behaviour. In measuring GLP it is hoped to find an indicator of how adaptable a person is or might be, how well he or she will act or function within a social system including language use (and non-verbal means of interaction). The language side of communication is thought to be highly dependent on the development of what might be termed the **language processing mechanisms** in general. In terms of information theory the GLP factor is considered by its proponents to represent something like the central core of human cognition, a person's executive programme governing all sub-routines and their coordination: linguistic, pragmatic etc. The fundamental problem involved here is, of course, that it cannot be determined with any degree of certainty what human cognition is made up of, how it functions, what cognitive abilities are implied in language learning and language use, whether an individual's performance in different languages (eg L1 and L2 or different L2) is governed by the same underlying cognitive factor or factors. As interesting as Oller's proposal of an analogy between perception and production of language is, as stimulating as the idea of language production as 'a kind of synthesis-by-analysis' (Oller 1978: 45) and the construct of an expectancy grammar as a whole may be – all of these thoughts are highly speculative and just a bit too sloppy for real life decisions to be based upon them. Neisser, for example, after having suggested in 1967 that speech is perceived by 'analysis-by-synthesis' no longer believes that this can be literally true: 'The listener's active constructions must be more open and less specific, so that they are rarely disconfirmed' (Neisser 1976: 32). Cognitive operations in language production are even less understood. Generally speaking, human cognition seems to be a much broader capacity than its language - specific : manifestation may make us believe.

I do not say, however, that language proficiency doesn't have anything to do with cognitive abilities and processes. It certainly does! There is hardly any doubt that language proficiency (in L1 as well as in L2) strongly relates to IQ and to different aspects of academic achievement. The decisive question is whether or not this is only one dimension of language proficiency (related to general cognitive and academic skills) or whether or not language proficiency is basically defined by the central core and can thus be called 'global'. Spolsky in 1975 stated that the ability to operate in a language only '**includes** a good, solid central portion' (Jones/Spolsky 1975: 69; emphasis by H J V). In a recently published article Cummins distinguishes between 'a convincing weak form and a less convincing strong form of Oller's arguments' (1979: 198; cf his proposed terms 'cognitive/academic language ability' (CALP) and 'basic interpersonal communicative skills' (BICS)). Cummins tries to prove that everybody acquires BICS in a first language and that CALP and BICS are also independent of one another in L2. I find his contribution quite useful – it is another piece of evidence against the unitary competence hypothesis (the strong form of Oller's claim).

163

3 The dynamics of language proficiency

Speaking of language proficiency as a generalised cognitive ability sounds very much as if we were thinking of it as a fixed state or the end product of development, if not even as a personality trait. This is especially true in its German translation where GLP could mean 'Stand der Sprachbeherrschung', but as much 'Allgemeine Sprachfähigkeit' closely associated (at least connotatively) with terms like 'Begabung' or 'Intelligenz' (in the sense of a quality that is either innate or, after having been acquired somehow, is considered to be rather stable). In this particular context we cannot take seriously enough a criticism developed by the sociological school of the Symbolic Interactionism against the traditional trait concept and picked up by interactional psychology during the past few years. This criticism goes like this, that the unit of analysis in the behavioural sciences cannot be the structure of human capabilities (the assumed stable 'traits') but will have to be the interrelationship between task situation and persons involved. This understanding of human behaviour goes well together with what has been the outcome so far of second language acquisition research along the lines of the **interlanguage hypothesis.** According to this theory language is acquired (in a natural setting) or learned (through formal instruction) in terms of a creative construction process which is more or less open-ended in the direction towards a native speaker's competence (target language). Proficiency then is interpreted as a dynamic construct, as the relative degree or level of competence a person has reached by the time of measurement. This competence, though, cannot be developed *ad infinitum,* as some researchers believe. Much discussion has been devoted therefore to the concept of **fossilisation** during the past years. This phenomenon, however, seems to be dependent on so many variables (cf Selinker/Lamandella 1978) that, for the time being, we have to assume that (almost) everyone can further develop his/her linguistic code and thus language proficiency under favourable circumstances — either by being trained or by finding the language system at hand not functional any more for one's social and personal needs (for discussion of this point cf Sampson 1978). On the other hand, linguistic knowledge apparently can just as easily be forgotten (or 'decomposed') in the process of not wanting or not having to use it.

By and large it seems justified to consider foreign language acquisition and language use as a dynamic process. Testing language proficiency means making a cut at a given point in time in order to form a more or less rough idea of a person's state of advancement. In view of the dynamics of language development it will indeed be advisable to test proficiency not only once, but (wherever possible) time and again. We should use different versions of the same measurement instrument as well as different methods altogether (one of the reasons being to control the effect of measurement method). In spite of all the statistical problems involved here I am quite convinced that each single measurement will add to the information we might already have of a person's language ability. It is very unlikely, indeed, that a single type of test will reflect any full assessment of the facets of language command (this human faculty which is very intricate and complex). In this respect I strongly agree with Ingram (1978) and Farhady (1979), and with Davies (1978), for that matter.

Some empirical considerations

Despite the fact that I have almost run out of space I would now like to add a few comments on the empirical side of the problem under consideration. To put it very crudely, neither one of the two opposing hypotheses about the structure of language ability has strong empirical evidence in its favour. In our research project at the Max-Planck-Institut für Bildungsforschung in Berlin we were able to show that the factor analytic studies done in support of the multidimensional model of language competence are by no means convincing as to the methods used and their interpretation of the statistical results. They do not offer a clear picture at all; one could say they tend to discourage the strong version of the divisible competence hypothesis (that each of the four skills is based upon a separate underlying factor with little or no interrelation at all)[3]. Yet many questions remain open (for example, as to number and nature of tests included etc.). On the whole the results cannot be simply ignored or done away with as being irrelevant (cf Vollmer/Sang forthcoming).

Likewise the empirical evidence presented in favour of the unitary competence hypothesis, when being re-evaluated, turns out to be by far not as strong and clear-cut as had been asserted by its proponents. For example, in some of the factor analyses presented there is indeed only one factor (within the limits of a sufficient eigenvalue) which can justly be taken as a general factor (cf Oller 1976). In other studies, however, a number of

---

[3] This is supported by Hosley and Meredith (1979) in a recent study on the structure of the construct of English proficiency, as measured by the TOEFL. According to their data the divisible competence hypothesis could be rejected. Instead of adopting the unitary competence hypothesis, however, they suggest a 'hierarchical skills theory' for consideration, which seems to be 'compatible with, but not derivable from, the present data' (1979: 217).

factors showed up (cf Oller/Hinofotis 1976; Scholz *et al* 1977), and I can't I quite understand why the unitary competence hypothesis should be the best explanation fitting these results (for further details see Sang/Vollmer 1978; Vollmer/Sang forthcoming).

As to our own research results a strong first factor (being the only one worthy of interpretation) emerged. But to our understanding the appearance of this factor could not be easily interpreted as an indication of the existence of a global language proficiency in the sense of the strong form of this argument (cf Sang/Vollmer 1978 and forthcoming).

I am afraid I'll have to go into factor analysis and testing theory just a bit more to make my point clearer. To cut things short, it is most important to make a clear distinction between what was later labelled the 'principal component model' on the one side and factor analysis in the narrower sense on the other side ('principal factor model'). In the latter model, according to Spearman's theory, factors represent either that portion of the variables under study which they have in common with other variables (so-called **common factors**) or that portion which they share with no others (so-called **unique factors**). In addition to a single general common factor which all tests included in his analysis would load high on, Spearman expected to see a number of unique factors on each of which only one of his tests had a substantial loading and the remaining tests a load of zero. Assuming that it is possible to concentrate the entire common variance of the tests on the general factor the residual correlations between the tests would then have to go to zero. Now up to this point researchers like Oller and Spearman are in agreement, at least in terms of their language. However their arguments begin to diverge when it becomes a matter of solving what is known as a problem of commonalities, ie determining the percentage of common variance. Here we run into a basic difference between the principal component model and the principal factor model.

Simply speaking the principal component model (the method used by Oller and by ourselves) doesn't even allow for the appearance of unique factors on top of the common factor expected. On the contrary, the principal component model produces one or more factors where each of the factors comprises common as well as unique variance in an indistinguishable manner. What we want, of course, is to have all the common variance concentrated on one factor whereas the others then only carry specificity. This is exactly what the principal factor model has been developed for and this is why it is superior to the other model.

But the problem with factor analysis is tougher yet when seen from a basic theoretical point of view. All classical forms of factor analysis including the ones mentioned so far are mostly used as **explorative methods,** that is to say, they work even without any piece of foregoing theory. All of these statistical procedures produce factors under almost any circumstances. We will never be able to select the meaningful factors from those that are pure artefacts. In other words, the structural hypothesis of a unitary factor, being the simplest under conditions given, has always quite a good chance of being confirmed, even if it does not represent at all any adequate description of the relationships among the several linguistic skills. Therefore we have to look for newer types of the so-called **'confirmatory' factor analysis** that allow a statistical comparison between theory-guided **structural predictions** and test results on the other hand. What we need is to expand our theoretical knowledge to a point enabling us to make precise **structural predictions** which are sound and reasonable. What we suggest in the end is the application of alternative research strategies: drawing the attention away from factor analysis as a seemingly convenient tool which doesn't help very much to solve the problems posed. Those alternative research strategies would mainly have to focus on language processing theory. They would have to throw light on those internal processes which determine a certain language behavior — preferably on experimental grounds. Here, of course, we touch on the question that many researchers are concerned with nowadays: it is the question of **construct validity** of those tests commonly used as indicators of general language competence[4]. We will never really understand what the correlations between tests of different skills mean, what they signify, and why some are higher than others — unless we better understand and are able to model more precisely the cognitive potentials and task specific operations on which performance in the various language tests depends. Only when our

---

[4] In this context it is interesting that the correlation between a Cloze test developed at Southern Illinois University and meant to be a measure of overall language proficiency on the one hand and an FSI-type oral interview on the other hand was no higher than .60, as reported in Jones (1977: 257; cf also Hinofotis 1980, where this correlation, however, is not mentioned any more at all). This moderate correlation with a speaking test suggests, I think, that at least speaking proficiency cannot be adequately predicted by a test of overall proficiency — or at least not as well predicted as the other skills. If that is true I cannot understand how anyone can conclude that the Cloze test could replace more complicated and more costly ESL testing procedures without substantial loss of information. I personally consider it to be really a substantial loss of information if we build our judgement of a person's general language proficiency on some measure which does not adequately represent his or her speaking ability. For me it would not be a valid measure of general language ability then.

theoretical knowledge increases, when we have moved further ahead towards construct validation, only then might factor analysis prove again to be useful under certain (restrictive) conditions.

Conclusion

After this excursion into methodological perspectives let me summarise my thoughts and then come back to the question: with all the dilemmas indicated, why are we (still) interested in 'General Language Proficiency'? I think the answer to this question has several aspects to it:

Proficiency testing has a **distinct social function** which has to do with 'future needs or control purposes', as Davies (1977: 46) so aptly put it. These social implications of proficiency measurement, their so-called predictive value, can be severe for any individual involved. For this very reason it is all the more important that we really understand what our judgement and prediction is based upon, that the construct is as valid as are the tests designed to assess it. If there is any doubt or any considerable degree of uncertainty as to what proficiency (in theoretical terms) really is or what proficiency tests really measure it would be irresponsible, in my opinion, to continue to use the construct (as if it were well defined)[5] or to administer any proficiency measure (as if we were sure about its validity) and use the test scores to make more or less irreversible decisions. There seems to be a certain tendency of many an administration to nourish the belief in the necessity and in the validity of proficiency testing. I would seriously question, however, many a case in which proficiency tests are being exploited for placement purposes or, even worse, career decisions to be based upon them. We should not take it for granted that proficiency testing is done worldwide: each single situation in which such cutting decisions on the basis of proficiency scores are said to be necessary should be questioned and the procedures applied should be publicly called for justification over and over again. We as a society on the whole simply cannot afford to classify people and divide them up (allotting educational and professional chances of

---

[5] In a very recently published article reviewing a number of proficiency tests used in the United States, Dieterich *et al* (1979) speak of 'the nebulous character of language proficiency' (1979: 547) in their conclusion.

different kinds) as long as the question of construct validity of the instruments used are not clarified somewhat further. This is especially true with the concept and measures of GLP[6].

I do not propose, of course, to do away with proficiency testing altogether, as some authors do. Proficiency measures are badly needed, for selection as well as for research purposes, and should therefore continue to be developed and improved (in terms of higher validity). However, as test designers, testers or testees alike we have to **bear in mind all the limiting conditions** that are yet connected with the concept of proficiency, especially again when it comes to overall proficiency. These uncertainties will have to show in the way we are interpreting test results as well as in the carefulness with which we are formulating conclusions or suggest decisions.

In any case, it seems necessary to use more than one type of test (or several sub-tests) in trying to assess so complex (and dubious) a thing as communicative competence (or language proficiency, if you like) — if it were only to make sure that we don't arrive at too narrow a view of a person's foreign language abilities and that our judgements are not unsound or made too quickly.

In addition, any proficiency measurement should not be done at a single point in time alone but should definitely be repeated under varying circumstances because in all probability each single measurement will add to our information and understanding of a person's language ability and language use. This is so even if we use different versions of the same measurement instrument. (The methodological problems involved here are left aside on purpose).

It has been argued in the past that this suggested procedure (more than one type of test plus repeated measurement) is uneconomical in a double sense: it is too expensive and too time-consuming. This objection is true, but the answer is: we have no other choice, things being as they are. Considerations

---

[6] A somewhat different attitude is expressed by Valette (1975) when she summarises her view on the need of prognostic instruments (especially referring to aptitude testing): 'Within the American educational framework, prognostic tests have but one legitimate use: to predict success in particular cases where an agency (governmental, industrial, etc.) needs to train a small number of personnel in a foreign language. Under such conditions, budget constraints and time factors demand that every effort be made to find the most suitable 'risks', that is, those candidates with the greatest chance of completing the course. Under such conditions, the fact that other equally suited candidates might be excluded due to the imperfections of the prognostic instrument is not a matter of concern since only a limited number of trainees are required in the first place' (1975: 10f.).

of practicality and/or money involved should — at least for a moment — be definitely kept apart from the question of validity (cf Stevenson, in press, for discussion of this point).

The notion of a GLPF and its strong form of interpretation by Oller and others that this dimension is unitary, representing the central core (in an absolute sense) of all that is meant by proficiency in a language (cf Cummins 1979), seems to be very seductive indeed. Apparently, it especially attracts the attention of administrative minds. To the, I believe, GLP is something like a handy label suggesting that the bothersome problems of evaluating people as to their language ability and making predictions as to their future behaviour and success could be solved easily now and effectively with a single instrument (which, admittedly, might need some more refinement, as the Cloze, for example). This is probably one of the main reasons why more and more people (teachers, administrators, managers of personnel) have become interested in GLP and how to assess it quickly (cf the rising awareness and demand for developing 'a' cloze test for English as a Foreign Language in the Federal Republic of Germany).

This perception of GLP implies — at least in my understanding — a good portion of wishful thinking. At the same time it has a strong affinity to the mentality of social engineering inasmuch as personal responsibility for evaluating other people, for making social judgements and decisions (all of them human acts than can be questioned, discussed and can potentially be revised, depending on the power structure) is hoped to be totally replaceable by 'objective' measures. It would be much easier to demonstrate (with the help of 'unquestionable' data) that certain people belong in certain categories, that the responsibility for any social (and socio-economic) consequences lies on the side of the testees themselves.

Fortunately, or unfortunately, things are not as clear-cut (yet). The notion of a GLP is in no way convincing so far, neither theoretically nor from an empirical point of view. The factor analytical data presented cannot be taken as strong evidence to support the unitary competence assumption. As a structural hypothesis it is much too general: a strong GLPF will always show up in statistical analysis explaining more or less of the common variance in a large number of L2 language measures. But the percentage of variance explained differs from study to study and, on the whole, is not high enough to be satisfied with (assuming, by the way, that all the tests included are reliable and valid). After having extracted the first factor (interpreted as GLPF) we cannot be sure at all that the remaining variance is nothing but unique and error variance. On the contrary, some factor analytic studies have indicated that there might be several common factors. As small as this counter evidence may be, it can definitely not be neglected.

Therefore, our search for more than one common factor underlying language performance will have to go on.

Wherever 'global language proficiency' in terms of Oller's strong claim is asserted to be measured we should be very sceptical. It may even be appropriate for some of us being test researchers to inform and back up examinees who begin to question the validity of language proficiency measures in general and demand explanation and justification of what they went through, why, and how exactly judgements were found and decisions arrived at. This may be a nightmare to many a tester and may certainly complicate the testing business — but that's what it is anyway: complicated and highly explosive in its social implications.

Editor's note: This is a revised version of a paper first presented at the First International Language Testing Symposium, held at the Bundessprachenamt, Hürth, 29 - 31 July 1979. The proceedings have since been published in KLEIN-BRALEY, C and STEVENSON, D K, eds. *Practice and problems in language testing, 1* (Bern and Frankfurt am Main: Lang, 1981).

BIBLIOGRAPHY

CANALE, M and SWAIN, M
Theoretical bases of communicative approaches to second language teaching and testing. Toronto: Ontario Institute for Studies in Education, 1979.

CARROLL, J B
Fundamental considerations in testing for English Language proficiency of foreign students. In: Testing the English proficiency of foreign students. Washington, DC: Center for Applied Linguistics, 1961. *Reprinted in:* ALLEN, H B, and CAMPBELL, R N, *eds.* Teaching English as a second language: a book of readings. 2nd ed. New York: McGraw-Hill, 1972, pp 313-321.

CARROLL, J B
The psychology of language testing. In: DAVIES, A *ed.* Language testing symposium: a psycholinguistic approach. London: Oxford University Press, 1968, pp 46-69.

CUMMINS, J
Cognitive/academic language proficiency, linguistic interdependence, the optimum age question and some other matters. In: Working papers on bilingualism, *19,* 197-205, 1979.

DAVIES, A
The construction of language tests. In: ALLEN, J P B, and DAVIES, A, *eds.* Testing and experimental methods. (The Edinburgh Course in Applied Linguistics, Vol 4) Oxford University Press, 1977, pp 38-104.

DAVIES, A
Language testing. In: Language teaching and linguistics abstracts, *11,* 145-159 and 215-231, 1978.

DIETERICH, T G, FREEMAN, C and CRANDALL, J A
A linguistic analysis of some English proficiency tests. In: TESOL Quarterly, *13,* 535-550, 1979.

FARHADY, H
The disjunctive fallacy between discrete-point and integrative tests. In: TESOL Quarterly, *13,* 347-357, 1979.

FODOR, J A, BEVER, T G, and GARRETT, M F
The psychology of language: an introduction to psycholinguistics and generative grammar. New York: McGraw-Hill, 1974.

HARRIS, D P
Testing English as a second language. New York: McGraw-Hill, 1969.

HINOFOTIS, F B
Cloze as an alternative method of ESL placement and proficiency Testing. (Paper presented at the annual meeting of the Linguistic Society of America, Philadelphia, 1976) *In:* OLLER, J W, Jr, and PERKINS, K *eds.* Research in language testing. Rowley, Massachusetts: Newbury House, 1980, pp 121 - 128.

HOSLEY D, and MEREDITH, K
Inter- and intra-test correlates of the TOEFL. In: TESOL Quarterly, *13,* 209-217, 1979.

INGRAM, E
The psycholinguistic basis. In: SPOLSKY, B, *ed.* Approaches to language testing. (Advances in language testing series 2) Arlington, Virginia: Center for Applied Linguistics, 1978, pp 1-14.

JONES, R L
Testing: a vital connection. In: PHILLIPS, J K, *ed.* The language connection: from the classroom to the world. (ACTFL foreign language education series 9) Skokie, Illinois: National Textbook Company, 1977, pp 237-365.

JONES, R L and SPOLSKY, B, eds
Testing language proficiency. Arlington, Va.: Center for Applied Linguistics, 1975.

NEISSER, U
Cognitive psychology. New York: Appleton-Century-Crofts, 1967.

NEISSER, U
Cognition and reality: principles and implications of cognitive psychology. San Francisco: Freeman, 1976.

OLLER, J W, Jr
Expectancy for successive elements: key ingredient to language use. In: Foreign language annals, *7,* 443-452, 1974.

173

OLLER, J W, Jr
Evidence for a general language proficiency factor: an expectancy grammar. In: Die Neueren Sprachen, *75,* 165-174, 1976.

OLLER, J W, Jr
Pragmatics and language testing. In: SPOLSKY, B, *ed.* Approaches to language testing. (Advances in language testing series 2) Arlington, Virginia: Center for Applied Linguistics, 1978, pp 39-57.

OLLER, J W, Jr, and HINOFOTIS, F B
Two mutually exclusive hypotheses about second language ability: factor-analytic studies of a variety of language tests. (Paper presented at the annual meeting of the Linguistic Society of America, Philadelphia, 1976) *Published with a different subtitle* ('Indivisible or partially divisible competence') *in:* OLLER, J W, Jr, and PERKINS, K, *eds.* Research in language testing. Rowley, Massachusetts: Newbury House, 1980, pp. 13-23.

OLLER, J W, Jr and PERKINS, K
eds. Research in language testing. Rowley, Massachusetts: Newbury House, 1980.

SAMPSON, G P
A model of second language learning. In: Canadian modern language review, *34,* 442-454, 1978.

SANG, F and VOLLMER, H J
Allgemeine Sprachfähigkeit und Fremdsprachenerwerb: zur Struktur von Leistungsdimensionen und linguistischer Kompetenz des Fremd-sprachenlerners. Berlin: Max-Planck-Institut für Bildungsforschung, 1978.

SANG, F and VOLLER, H J
(forthcoming) *Modelle linguistischer Kompetenz und ihre empirische Fundierung. In:* GROTJAHN, R and HOPKINS, E, *eds.* Empirical research on language teaching and language acquisition. (Quantitative linguistic series) Bochum: Studienverlag Dr Brockmeyer.

SCHOLZ, G and others
Is language ability divisible or unitary? A factor analysis on twenty-two English proficiency tests. (Paper presented at the 11th Annual TESOL Convention, Miami, Florida, 1977) *Published in:* OLLER, J W, Jr, and PERKINS, K, *eds.* Research in language testing. Rowley, Massachusetts: Newbury House, 1980, pp 24-33.

SELINKER, L and LAMANDELLA, J T
Fossilisation in interlanguage learning. In: BLATCHFORD, C H and
SCHACHTER, J, *eds.* On TESOL '78: EFL policies, programmes,
practices. Washington, DC: Teachers of English to speakers of other
languages. 1978, pp 240-249.

SPOLSKY, B
*What does it mean to know a language? or how do you get someone to
perform his competence? In:* OLLER, J W, Jr, and RICHARDS, J C,
eds. Focus on the learner: pragmatic perspectives for the language teacher.
Rowley, Massachusetts: Newbury House, 1973, pp 164-176.

STEVENSON, D K (in press)
*Beyond faith and face validity: the multitrait-multimethod matrix and
the convergent and discriminant validity of oral proficiency tests.* (Paper
delivered at the Colloquium on the Validation of Oral Proficiency Tests
at the 13th Annual TESOL Convention, Boston, 1979) *In:* PALMER, A S,
and GROOT, P J M, *eds.* The validation of oral proficiency tests.
Washington, DC: Teachers of English to speakers of other languages.

STRAIGHT, H S
Comprehension versus production in linguistic theory. In: Foundations of
language, *14,* 525-540, 1976.

VALETTE, R M
Modern language testing: a handbook. New York: Harcourt Brace
Jovanovich, 1967.

VALETTE, R M
Directions in foreign language testing. New York: New York: Modern
Language Association, 1975.

VOLLMER, H J and SANG, F
*Zum psycholinguistischen Konstrukt einer internalisierten
Erwartungsgrammatik.* Trier: Linguistic Agency, University of Trier
(LAUT), Series B, No 46, 1979.

VOLLMER, H J and SANG, F (forthcoming)
*Competing hypotheses about second language ability: a plea for caution.
Submitted for publication in:* Applied psycholinguistics.

REACTION TO THE PALMER & BACHMAN AND
THE VOLLMER PAPERS (1)

Arthur Hughes, University of Reading

My immediate reaction to the these two papers was the strong feeling that I needed to put them aside and work out for myself just what was involved in claims made about unitary competence and general language proficiency. I must confess that I have not always been sure what was being claimed, with what justification, and at times I have even wondered whether anything very interesting was being said at all. This paper is an account of the thinking that has helped me reduce my uncertainty. It also makes suggestions for the improvement of research in the area. I shall make points and present arguments as briefly as possible, allowing the discussion to provide whatever expansion is necessary.

We say that someone is proficient at something when he can perform certain tasks to what we regard as an acceptable standard.[1] So it is with language proficiency, though our notion of adequacy is as likely to be norm-referenced as it is criterion-referenced. The question arises immediately: what are the relevant tasks for the assessment of language proficiency? The answer is that we are at liberty to choose whatever language-based tasks we like: solving anagrams, finding rhymes, judging the grammaticality or acceptability of sentences, making translations, or even doing cloze tests. It seems to me, however, that certain tasks — such as reading a book with understanding, writing a letter, or holding a conversation — are more central to our interests. The uses of the four skills in performing more or less natural language functions is, after all, what most modern language teaching supposedly has as its objective. It follows from this that the study of the performance of such tasks is an essential part of research into language proficiency, just as it is against such performance that proficiency tests must be validated. It is not good enough to administer the writing ability section of TOEFL, which once correlated at around .7 with some writing task but which is essentially a test of the grammar appropriate to formal English, and then claim that you have measured writing ability.

---

[1] Vollmer worries whether proficiency is a matter of competence or performance. The distinction is unnecessary. We might use it if we thought it helped us think more clearly about the matter in hand, but I believe that, at least if it is the Chomskyan distinction(s) we have in mind, it does quite the opposite.

The 'natural' language tasks that most concern us can be classified according to:

1 which skill or skills (of the four) are involved
2 subject matter
3 style
4 regional variety
5 function

and, doubtless(6) something you have thought of that I have omitted. There are thus in principle a great many proficiencies. We ought not to need experiments like that of Bachman and Palmer to tell us that, even when measures are norm-referenced, individuals do not show equal ability in each of them. How then is the unitary competence hypothesis (UCH) to be defended? Presumably by pointing out:—

1 The individual will have had unequal exposure to or practice in the different skills, styles etc. You are unlikely to speak English very well if you have never heard it, however much you have read it. Nor will you understand British English as well as American English when you have previously only heard the latter. The unitary competence hypothesis must assume, then, equal exposure and practice. (Even though proficiency tests are thought of as looking forwards rather than backwards, if they were genuinely intended to predict longer-term future (rather than tomorrow's) performance, they would have to take into account previous exposure and practice (or some measure of aptitude)). Research must control for, or at least take into account, exposure and practice.

2 Non-linguistic factors will inhibit performance in some tasks but not others. These may be of two kinds:—

a emotional or cultural; like shyness or excessive respect. For the tester, provided the inhibition is more or less permanent and not just a product of the testing situation, inferior performance may be considered to give a true picture of the subject's ability. For the researcher interested in the UCH, on the other hand, it can be argued that differences attributable to such factors are of no significance, and must be controlled for.

b some physical defect; poor eyesight, cleft palate. Because the eyes and mouth are at the periphery of the language processing system(s), they may be dismissed as non-linguistic and irrelevant to the UCH. The temptation will be, however, to regard as irrelevant anything which results in a difference in performance between skills; for example, differences between visual and auditory memory which might well contribute to differences between reading and listening ability. If this line is pursued far enough (something which the competence-performance distinction encourages), anything which language processes do not have in common will be excluded from consideration, and the UCH will inevitably be substantiated.

If we ignore differences in performance attributable to (1), (2, a), and those parts of (2, b) that we think reasonable, would we expect performance in the different skills to be equivalent (with norm-referencing)? Our expectations might depend on what we know about (1) language processing, and (2) such learner variables as (a) aptitude and (b) motivation.

1   The first thing to say about language processing is that we know very little about it (see Butterworth (1980) for recent confessions of psycholinguists). One can, however, indulge in conjecture. It would be strange, I suppose, if there were (at least) four completely independent processing systems. To the degree that we monitor our speech, speaking and listening processes are presumably related. And when one skill is firmly established before the development of another is begun, a parasitic relationship between them seems inevitable (for example, my subject Blanca (Hughes 1979) had still read no English after 6 months learning of the language through conversation with me; yet she was able to read immediately I presented her with a book). At the same time, psycholinguists would seem to be moving towards the view that each process is sufficiently different to necessitate quite separate study, something reflected in the nature of books recently published in the field.

In the end, part of our understanding of the nature of language proficiency will be in terms of language processes. But the end is not near, and I agree with Vollmer that we should be sceptical of explanations that make use of concepts like 'synthesis by analysis'.

2   a   Even if relatively independent processes are involved in the four skills, equivalent performance in each could result from differences in language aptitude. Aptitude for one skill might be a perfect predictor of aptitude for the other three. Evidence (perhaps not particularly reliable) from Pimsleur et al and Gardner and Lambert, however, would point to this not being the case.

Obviously language processes and aptitude are related; the aptitude we are talking about is for developing these processes. Nevertheless, similarity of processes and aptitude are logically distinct explanations of apparent unitary competence. Oller has spoken about both, without, as far as I know, presenting them as alternatives. I would suggest that a full understanding of language proficiency will be facilitated by (and may depend on) further research into aptitude.

b Similarities and differences in performance between skills might be due to different degrees and types of motivation for the possession of these skills. Gardner and Lambert's (1972) work would suggest that this is a line of research worth pursuing, using more sophisticated measuring techniques.

I said earlier that we must get subjects to perform a variety of 'genuine' language tasks. What I want to add now is that we should measure performance on each task according to as many criteria as possible. It is essential, I think, that judgements should be independent; judges A B C would rate according to one criterion and no other. Where a single judge is required to provide ratings according to a number of criteria, a high correlation between them seems inevitable (eg FSI interview in Oller and Hinofotis, which results in a separate factor).

While on the subject of the conduct of experiments in this field, I want to suggest that the subjects be of as limited a range of ability within which it is possible to discriminate reliably. Too wide a range will bias the results in favour of the UCH, obscuring interesting and important differences. It is no surprise that when the ability range in Oller and Hinofotis's (1980) experiment was reduced, another factor emerged.

I have talked so far about the four skills and varieties. The other dimension of proficiency along which separable components have been thought to lie is the linguistic: grammar, semantics (or vocabulary), phonology/graphology. However plausible such components may seem, it must be remembered that levels are for the convenience of linguistic description and theory, and while some correspondence with units or stages of processing seem plausible, a one-to-one relationship is by no means inevitable. What is more, within linguistics there is not always agreement on the number and nature of the levels appropriate to descriptions of particular languages.

Even when there is agreement, it is clear that levels are not discrete, that they interact eg phonology and syntax in English negative contraction. In language learning there are similar interactions, for example Rodgers' (1969) finding that success with which items of Russian vocabulary were learned depended largely on the ease with which their phonetic shape allowed them to be anglicised. And the difficulties error analysts experience (or should experience) in assigning errors to levels are well known.

In the light of what has been said in the previous paragraph it would not be surprising if it proved impossible to separate out these linguistic components when evaluating performance on various linguistic tasks and to establish them as factors underlying performance on all the tasks. But I do think it is worth trying, provided that 'real' language tasks are involved and that the supplementary tests meant to measure control of the separate components are 'pure' (I am thinking of vocabulary items in the grammar sections of the English Language Battery (Edinburgh) and the English Placement Test (Michigan). Judgments of performance might be supplemented by linguistic analysis (eg types of structure used/misused in written and spoken output).

It should be clear, I think, from what has gone before, that I regard most of the research that has been done in this area as deficient in one respect or another. Few conclusions can be safely drawn. Interesting work **can** be done, but it must be more carefully controlled, using more or less homogeneous groups performing 'real' language tasks (amongst others). Whatever is done, I fear that it will be a long time before progress in the study of language processing will be sufficient to improve significantly the quality of language proficiency tests; and factorial studies of language performance are unlikely to provide more than clues as to the nature of language processes. What promises to bring more immediate benefits, at least to tests, is the continued investigation of the relationships holding between performance on a variety of language tasks. Whatever the fate of the UCH, if it continues to stimulate worthwhile research it will have done that much good.

BIBLIOGRAPHY

BUTTERWORTH, B
ed. *Language production* (Volume 1, Speech and talk) London:
Academic Press, 1980.

GARDNER, R C and LAMBERT, W E
Attitudes and motivation in second-language learning. Rowley,
Massachusetts: Newbury House, 1972.

HUGHES, A
Aspects of a Spanish adult's acquisition of English. In: Interlanguage
studies bulletin (Utrecht), 4 1, 1979.

OLLER, J W Jr, and HINOFOTIS, F B
*Two mutually exclusive hypotheses about second language ability:
indivisible or partially divisible competence.* In: OLLER, J W, Jr and
PERKINS, K. Research in language testing. Rowley, Massachusetts:
Newbury House, 1980.

OLLER, J W Jr, and PERKINS, K
Research in language testing. Rowley: Massachusetts: Newbury House,
1980.

PIMSLEUR, P, SUNDLAND, D M and McINTYRE, R D
Underachievement in foreign language learning. In: IRAL, 2 2, 1964.

RODGERS, T S
*On measuring vocabulary difficulty: an analysis of item variables in
learning Russian-English vocabulary pairs.* In: IRAL, 7, 327-343, 1969.

REACTION TO THE PALMER & BACHMAN AND THE VOLLMER PAPERS (2)

Alan Davies, University of Edinburgh

The general versus specific (or unitary versus divisible) competence debate is a classic of psychology and no doubt of philosophy too. It has, like all great disputes, traces of the grand and unsolvable binary themes, of nature versus nurture and realism versus nominalism and perhaps good versus evil. My own view is that the structure of competence or skills or ability is partly a practical issue and partly a mathematical choice. (Of course it is also a philosophical question but in this instance that seems to me not amenable to proof). From a practical point of view it is important whether one views language (or any other 'ability' or 'skill' or 'competence') as a whole or as an array of parts — the implications for syllabus, for testing and even for varying learner activities are obvious, as are the criteria for judging eventual success. The mathematical issue may be less obvious but it is a well-known chestnut of applied statistics, viz that in Factor Analysis 'solutions' there are (at least) two ways of presenting the results, either as a superordinate with several (possible) subordinates (Type A) or as a set of equal partners (Type B). The Principal Components method of Factor Analysis will typically produce a Type A solution, the Rotation method a Type B. The great exponents of Factor Analysis have indeed represented the Type A (Spearman's general factor, involving a hierarchy) and the Type B (Thurstone's group factors) solutions. But there is no way of preferring one method (and therefore solution) to the other, short of appeal to one's view of the universe or of arithmetic elegance.

My position, then, on the issue of General Language Proficiency (GLP) is that it is essentially a non-issue theoretically. At the same time the practical implications are important.

I will now consider some of the arguments in the two papers and then make some procedural suggestions. In both papers the authors refer to J W Oller whose work has renewed interest in the question of language test validity (essentially the question of what should one test and therefore of the structure of abilities — one or more factors) through empirical rather than speculative research. It must be said that the discussion over Oller's work, which he has fostered, has been on a slightly separate issue. Oller's data show that his integrative or as he says pragmatic tests eg dictation, cloze, represent total EFL proficiency better than any other single test or indeed combination of tests. Whether this is so or not it is **not** an argument for the unitary factor view since, as Oller would agree, both dictation and cloze are so integrative

that they contain most or all language abilities. Now, if you construct a test
that already contains everything you cannot then argue that it contains everything. So, as I see it, the 'best test' data and arguments of Oller are not
necessarily of relevance in the GLP debate. I will not, therefore, deal directly
with the Oller results, and turn first to Palmer and Bachman.

Here the two authors present results of a two-year study in construct
validation carried out by them but monitored and encouraged by participants
at two TESOL colloquia on oral tests in 1979 and 1980. The general method
employed was that of the multitrait-multimethod model. In this case the
design allowed for three Methods and two Traits, the methods being: interview, translation and self-ratings, and the traits: communicative competence
in reading and communicative competence in speaking. Apart from the
methodological interest of the project the aim was to investigate the validity
of the construct: communicative competence in speaking. Palmer and
Bachman assembled six tests (3 methods X 2 traits) which they administered
to an N of 75 non-native speakers at the University of Illinois. The results
are presented and discussed in the light of two methods of analysis, a
correlational analysis and a confirmatory factor analysis. (Note that the
third method they mention, principal component analysis, is not used,
apparently for reasons of bias).

I do not always see eye to eye with Palmer and Bachman about the nature of
correlation. For example, they say . . 'if a test of the trait "mathematical
ability" and another of the trait "verbal ability" always gave the same
results, that is if they ordered the subjects taking the tests in exactly the same
ways, there would be no evidence that the mathematical and verbal ability
traits were actually distinct'. While that is true, so is the converse, there
would be no evidence that they were **not** distinct. Correlations are indicators
of shared variance not or equivalent identity. Again, the kind of argument
used about correlation sizes makes me uneasy. Here is a typical example: 'The
effect of method is particularly noticeable in tests using translation or self-
rating methods. Of the indices, in the diagonal in the lower left-hand box the
intercorrelations between tests 3 — 5 which employ translation and self-rating
methods (.64, .69, and .68) are clearly higher than those between tests 1 and
2 which do not (.54 and .46)'. Apart from the lack of mention of reliability
of rs here and of any tests of significance between rs what is missing is the
recognition that eg the first two rs mentioned may represent different
segments of variance space ($.64^2 = .41$ and $.69^2 = .48$). Now it is difficult
enough to compare repeated rs of X on Y since until they reach .7 they may
occupy quite different variance space, but it is even more difficult with
rs between quite different pairs. To say that the r of X on Y is bigger than
the r of A on B is not necessarily very instructive.

I find in Palmer and Bachman another problem, that of distinguising clearly between Method and Trait. (I understand that this was an issue at the second colloquium in 1980). Palmer and Bachman select Communicative Competence in reading as a trait and translation as a method. But it could be maintained that translation is a trait and reading a method. Or better that they are both combinations of method and trait. No method it seems to me can ever be entirely free of the trait it seeks to realise. Interview, like translation, again seems to me as much trait as method. And so on. Only very technical 'methods' (like multiple-choice questioning) may be trait-free and I am not sure even about these. Next the arguments against Principal Component Factor Analysis. I don't understand these, either that PrinComp can be used only for variance structure and not covariance structure, or that 'principal component analysis cannot be used to examine any kind of structural model in which the elements in the model are correlated . . .' Why not? Surely most factor analysis studies deal with correlated elements.

Notice that in terms of correlations (Table 1) both for reading and speaking it is self-rating that is the 'best' method in that it shares least with the other methods. What that argument indicates is the slight absurdity of comparing correlation sizes.

In spite of my animadversions it seems to me that Palmer and Bachman do demonstrate their hypothesis, *viz* that **according to their analysis** the two traits, reading and speaking, differ when method is controlled.

The issues raised by Palmer and Bachman are arithmetical ones, they have to do with differing interpretations of factor analysis. Vollmer presents us with a different kind of argument. In the first place, Vollmer is deliberately offering a critique of the GLP position. In the second place, he advances his arguments from a theoretical standpoint. (He tells us that he has supporting data but does not in this paper present them.) What, he asks, can GLP be a description of? Is it about competence or about performance? Is it a metaphor, a way of talking about language ability; is it a construct (like competence) which enables us to idealise language itself? (He recognises that this implies some static nonvarying view of language ability.) Or is it an argument about language skills (ie performance)? If that then it would be possible to combine in one's view of language ability both GLP (= competence) and the divisible view (ie performance), though of course empirically we might find that in performance too the GLP position could be maintained.

Vollmer points out that the divisible competence hypothesis has been assumed by 'a great number of researchers' who have adopted this view for want of a convincing theoretical alternative. So while there is no (or little) experimental evidence for this view there is a lot of experience and, as

Vollmer indicates, many of our assumptions belong to this divisible competence position. At the same time there has always been the related assumption of 'transfer ability', *viz* that there is the likelihood of performance on one test being substantially correlated with performance on another.

Vollmer then shows how the concept of 'overall proficiency' has inevitably merged into the second major hypothesis, that of a unitary competence. Vollmer's position is that this unitary competence view, widely promoted by eg Oller in his discussion of an 'internalised expectancy grammar' is not justified and that it flies in the face of substantial evidence in favour of two competencies (at least), those related to comprehension and production.

Vollmer characterises the central idea of GLP as a psychological construct, identified in some way with the 'general cognitive apparatus' of a person. The trouble with this view, Vollmer suggests, is that it fails to incorporate the necessary dynamic of L2 proficiency, a dynamic which is captured by eg the interlanguage hypothesis.

From his own empirical studies Vollmer claims that neither the unitary nor the divisible hypothesis has strong grounds for acceptance. Vollmer points to the differing but equivalent solutions provided by Factor Analysis and concludes that for all known practical (especially selectional) situations a GLP construct is dangerous and altogether too simple. What is needed, Vollmer suggests, is more theoretical work on construct validity. Which takes us back full circle to Palmer and Bachman who, it will be remembered, start from a construct validity hypothesis and then carry out empirical research to test that hypothesis. So far so good.

Finally, I want to make a suggestion as to how we might approach the GLP issue by indicating the different kinds of argument involved. First, there is the **philosophical argument**: this may be what is meant by construct validity if it allows for testing. Thus the argument that GLP applies to both L1 and L2 seems to me interesting and testable. The argument that speaking and reading in an L2 are/are not combined in a GLP is, as Palmer and Bachman show, testable. Second there is the **competence-performance** argument. Since this is **either** a philosophical **or** a practical issue (ie we are testing one or the other) this merges into one of the other arguments. Third, there is the **practical** argument which is well considered by Vollmer and which says in view of our lack of clarity it is best to gather as much evidence as possible from a wide variety of tests; this has special force in diagnostic testing. Fourth, there is the **factor analysis** argument, though this does seem to produce conflicting results. Important arguments that are not much discussed are those dealing with **language variation** (Vollmer mentions this through time — his dynamic — but what of inter-speaker variation: whose GLP are we talking about?), with **predictive validity** and with the **'one best test'** idea, integrative, communicative or pragmatic.

REPORT OF THE DISCUSSION ON GENERAL LANGUAGE PROFICIENCY

J Charles Alderson, University of Lancaster

Preamble

The debate about the unitary competence hypothesis revolves around the issue: is there one underlying proficiency in a second language, or are there several proficiencies, which are separately measurable and teachable? Is Reading separate from Writing or Listening? Is knowledge of vocabulary distinct and separable from knowledge of grammar? If there are no differences between these 'knowledges' or 'skills' (or at least demonstrable differences), the practical consequences are quite considerable, namely that one only needs to measure 'proficiency', and the test used is relatively unimportant. The pedagogic consequence seems to be that one need not worry about teaching, say, writing and speaking explicitly, since teaching reading alone will affect general language proficiency and, 'automatically', writing will improve. Of course, the existence of a general language proficiency factor could also be used to justify the opposite of concentrating on teaching reading in order to improve reading ability: in order to improve reading it might be argued, one can validly teach the writing, speaking and listening skills at the same time, since they all relate to General Language Proficiency.

It was apparent during the discussion of this topic that there was a problem of level of abstraction or generalisation in the identification or acceptance of the existence of one general language proficiency factor: since all humans have language, in one sense at least there can only be one general language proficiency factor underlying Language. General Language Proficiency (GLP) from such a perspective is what language is. The more interesting discussion starts when one looks at less abstract levels: at such levels it is self-evident that people have different skills: some people can speak and understand when spoken to, but cannot write or read acceptable English. Other people have merely a reading knowledge of a language, and are unable to write it, speak it or understand the spoken form of it. However, these differences would be more apparent than real if there is a common underlying competence.

When someone is proficient, we mean that s/he can perform a task, any task, to a required level (the criterion). If an individual is given several tasks to perform and he performs them differently, does this mean that he has differing abilities (proficiencies)? Would one, in any case, expect performances in the different skill areas of a second language to be

187

equivalent? It was suggested in the debate that given the vast variety of sociolinguistic settings in which it is possible to perform in a second language, one would surely anticipate a variety of different proficiencies underlying performances on various tasks. Common sense suggests that we do not **need** empirical research of the Bachman and Palmer or Oller kind to prove the obvious. Curiously, however, research results, particularly those based on principal component and factor analyses do not always show the different proficiencies one expects.

One view was that the reason for this might be the method of analysis: the statistical method one chooses conditions the results one gets. Principal Component Analysis is intended to simplify data, to reduce it to one best solution if possible, and is therefore likely to result in one factor emerging from the intercorrelations of, for example, a battery of apparently different language tests. Maximum likelihood factor analysis on the other hand, looks for as many factors underlying the data as possible, and tests emerging factors for significant contributions to variance. That the number of factors one discovers may be an artefact of one's statistical model is suggested also by a study by Oller and Hinofotis (1980). A given set of data was analysed according to the principal component method, and one factor was revealed. When the data was factor analysed using a Varimax rotation procedure, two factors emerged, one relating to FSI interviews, and the other to cloze and multiple-choice test performance. In order to disprove the General Language Proficiency hypothesis, clearly the method of analysis one selects should not be the one which **favours** the hypothesis. It was generally agreed that in research of this kind one should always use maximum likelihood factor analysis.

It was suggested that another reason for the failure of several factors to emerge from the data may be the lack of homogeneity of the groups studied. Studies have suggested that when a relatively homogeneous subgroup of a population is studied, more factors emerge than when one looks at the heterogeneous population. It was not, however, entirely clear in the discussion why this should be. The claim is that to allow interesting differences among individuals to emerge, one needs to study a relatively homogeneous group, ie to allow the maximum possibility for several factors in language proficiency. But this does not seem to be reconcilable with the consideration of differences in performance: if the sample studied included people with deformities, for example, or gross differences in length of exposure to the second language, that would increase the likelihood of more than one factor emerging. Thus increased heterogeneity should lead to a multi-factor solution. Should one exclude from one's sample such extreme differences in performance? If so, when do differences in performance cease to be 'extreme'? When the results they yield prove our hypothesis? This, it was felt, was unsatisfactory.

The argument that heterogenous groups lead to a (false) unifactorial solution was illustrated with an example. Assume that Tom, Dick and Harry form a heterogeneous group with respect to language proficiency, such that Tom is much better than Dick, who in turn is much better than Harry. If one attempted to see whether there are separate abilities in, say, writing and listening, with such a group, one would find that Tom was better than Dick in both writing and listening, and Dick was better than Harry in both abilities also. Thus only one factor **could** emerge from such a group, given the constant rank order of subjects. Yet interesting differences might exist between Tom's writing and listening abilities, and simply be obscured. The important question, is: if we are interested in differences within one individual, why do we group individuals together at all? Doing so is quite likely to obscure differences, unless the differences within individuals are the same for all or most individuals (which may not be likely). To put the argument graphically, it might be found from test data that individual T. has a profile of various abilities (test scores) that looks like:

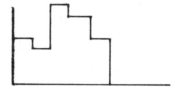

Whereas individual H. has a profile that looks like:

That is, both appear to have interesting differences in abilities. However, if one groups the scores, the result is:

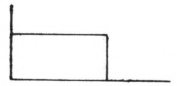

One might argue that one wants data from groups rather than individuals for reasons of realiability. One might also be interested in comparability: Harry's writing may be worse than his listening **and** that is true for everybody else also, which is an interesting fact. Similarly, of course, it is also interesting if Harry's writing is worse than his listening and such is **not** the case for anybody else.

Considerable discussion took place over the reasons for the interest in General Language Proficiency. Why is one at all interested in differences between writing and listening? What does one want to know? Do we want to know if different individuals merely find writing more difficult than listening? Or do we want to know whether there is a relationship between writing and listening? If there is a relationship, what are the consequences? Does the fact that one can perhaps predict listening ability from writing ability help us to produce better tests? Does it help us to understand language proficiency better? It was suggested that there are obvious teaching implications of such relationships, of the existence of one general language proficiency factor, or of several closely related proficiencies. There are also practical consequences for language testing of the existence of such relationships, or, indeed, of the existence of only one language proficiency. If there is only one general language proficiency, it may be argued that any language test that taps this proficiency will suffice. This, essentially, is the 'one best test' argument, put forward in relation to integrative test like cloze test and dictation tests. The argument is that there is such a high correlation between, say, a cloze test and a variety of other types of tests that for all practical purposes it does not matter whether one uses a variety of other tests, or the cloze test alone. The question raised was whether testers (and, more crucially, testees and teachers) are happy to test just one 'skill' knowing that it will tap the one general language proficiency factor to the same extent and with the same efficiency as any other test? Are we content to ignore writing and speaking in our tests (because they are difficult to test or impractical) since we 'know' we will measure the ability underlying Writing and Speaking with more practicable tests of listening and reading? It is commonly argued in favour of 'indirect' measurement of writing in, for example, the TOEFL that such measures correlate highly with more direct measures.

It was generally agreed that the only reasonable view to take on the 'One Best Test' argument must be that of Vollmer, namely that, regardless of the correlations, and quite apart from any consideration of the lack of face validity of the One Best Test, we must give testees a fair chance by giving them a **variety** of language tests, simply because one might be wrong: there might be no Best Test, or it might not be the one we chose to give, or there might not be **one** general language proficiency factor, there may be several. The one Best Test argument derives from the Unitary Competence Hypothesis, (since if competence is unitary, any test will measure it). It may be that the Unitary Competence hypothesis is too simple. The fact is that it is too dangerous at a practical level because it implies that it does not matter which test one uses, and that is unacceptable when decisions are being taken, on the basis of test data, which affect people's lives. There may be arguments for using a smaller number or a narrower range of language tests when it is not important that our measurements be accurate. In other words, our purpose in testing, and the consequences of making wrong decisions about people, will affect **what** testing we do, and how many tests we give, regardless of the posited existence of one general language proficiency factor. A related issue, already raised in the discussion of communicative language testing in connection with extrapolation, was also mentioned at this point. If one needs to predict how well someone will perform in a seminar discussion, does one have to measure **that** performance? If a cloze test will predict the performance, should we not be content with the cloze test? The problem with such an argument, apart from the ethical arguments already mentioned, is that it presupposes that we can actually measure seminar performance. This is precisely what communicative language testing attempts to do, but so far there has been little convincing success.

A doubt was expressed as to whether it is possible to say anything meaningful about the existence of one general language proficiency factor until we have investigated specific competences. It was claimed that in the UK typically we do not attempt to test general language proficiency by producing general language tests, but that there is a tradition of testing for specific purposes, and in particular for academic study purposes. The theoretical notion behind ESP testing is that there is no General Language Proficiency. There would appear to be a conflict between the proponents of the Unitary Competence Hypothesis and ESP testers, who would argue that one must identify the real, sociologically defined activities and skills, and measure them. Presumably, however, it **is** possible to investigate GLP without prior investigation of specific competences, at least in the sense of an ESP test, and that would be by looking at what people can do in the most context-free situation. R A Kelly, for example, in his tests for the Department of Education in Canberra, Australia, has attempted to limit content and context by taking real texts and substituting the lexical items with other lexical items and nonsense words, in an attempt to get at a general language proficiency. One's view of whether it is necessary to go to such lengths depends in part upon whether one believes that context **determines** meaning (a strong hypothesis which would lead one to reject work like Kelly's) or whether context merely **conditions** meaning (the weak hypothesis). One may wonder also whether it is **possible** to remove context from text, if one includes within context the knowledge and experience that the testee/reader/interlocutor brings to the text or communication. The search for non-specialised texts for Reading Comprehension tests (texts comprehensible to the educated lay person, for example) looks like an attempt to find neutral content. However, does not this very search presuppose the existence of a general language proficiency factor? We choose 'neutral' content for our general tests in order not to bias the test in favour of one type of knowledge or experience, yet we predict from performance on such a test to performance within a specific context — assuming thereby that there must be a general language factor underlying both performances. If it is unacceptable to assume that there is a general language proficiency factor, then are we not driven to ESP-type tests? Of course the reverse argument also holds: that if there is a general language proficiency factor, then text **content** does not matter, and one can predict from performance on one text to performance on any other text. If this is an unreasonable inference from the Unitary Competence Hypothesis, then presumably the hypothesis would appear to be untenable. It was not clear whether the alternative to the UCH meant positing the existence of different proficiencies or abilities for different types of texts, or one proficiency for familiar texts, and another one for unfamiliar texts, or one for general texts and one for specific texts. In addition, the relationship was unclear between the notion of a 'core language' — basic structures, key vocabulary, and so on — and the Unitary Competence Hypothesis. It was felt that the Unitary Competence Hypothesis necessarily required that there be a core language in which to be proficient.

A question was raised of the implications for test profiles, of the sort done by ELTS, of the existence of a general language proficiency factor. If there were only one general language proficiency, then profiles across different tests would not be necessary, or, conceivably, possible. It was not clear to what extent a general language proficiency factor would allow for differences in profiles, that is differences among individuals across a series of tests, regardless of the differing test difficulties.

It was agreed that if there were one general language proficiency **across** languages there would be important educational consequences. For example, it may be true that one's reading ability in a second language is affected (or determined) by one's reading ability in the first language — certainly the general language proficiency theory would suggest this. There would appear to be value in research which examined the relationship between reading abilities in the first and second languages, and, if possible, related that to levels of proficiency in the second language. The results of Alderson, Bastien and Madrazo (1977), Clark (1979) and Alderson (1980) would suggest that it is not impossible to investigate the Unitary Competence Hypothesis **across** languages, by hypothesising the existence of two factors, one in the first language and one in the second.

General agreement was reached that research was needed into a number of areas related to but not necessarily derived from the UCH. Research into the relationship between abilities in first and second language would, as suggested, be of practical interest. There is a need to develop tests of criterion behaviours and then to relate a series of relatively indirect tests to those criteria to determine their best predictors and the interrelationships among tests. Such information should not only help us to understand better the nature of language proficiency, and language performance, but also enable us to improve our language tests, and possibly facilitate the understanding of general principles to make tests more efficient. The method of such research would be to assemble a battery of potential predictors — all selected or constructed according to a theory of language processing and production — to relate them to each other and to create and develop a data bank of test relations and performances. Clearly, it would be as important to know which tests were unrelated to others, or which were unsuccessful predictors, as it would be to know which tests were related or predictive.

Similarly it is necessary to research the relationships between performance on a test with one type of subject content, and that on a similar test with different subject content. Such research would throw light on the relationship between general language proficiency and specific language proficiencies, and between general language tests and ESP-type tests. A suitable vehicle for such research might be the new ELTS tests, with similar reading tests in the six areas of Physical, Medical, Life and Social Sciences, Technology and General Academic Studies.

The importance of the Unitary Competence Hypothesis was felt to be at least as much its capacity to generate controversy and research as its inherent truth, or lack of it.

BIBLIOGRAPHY

ALDERSON, J C
L_2 Reading: A Reading Problem or a Language Problem?
Paper presented at TESOL Conference, San Francisco, USA, 1980.

ALDERSON, J C BASTIEN, S and MADRAZO, A M
A comparison of Reading Comprehension in English and Spanish.
Research and Development Unit Report Number 9, UID, CELE, UNAM,
Mexico: mimeo. (1977).

CLARKE, M
Reading in Spanish and English: Evidence from adult ESL students.
Language Learning, Vol. 29, No. 1, pp 121-150. (1979).

DAVIES, A
Language Testing: Survey Article. Linguistics and Language Teaching
Abstracts, Vol. 11, nos. 3/4, 1978.

DAVIES, A, MOLLER, A and ADAMSON, D
*The English Proficiency of Foreign Students in Higher Education
(Non-University) in Scotland.* A report to the Scottish Education
Department, Edinburgh.

EGGLESTON, J F, GALTON, M and JONES, M E
Science teaching observation schedule. (Science Council research
Studies) Macmillan Education, 1975.

KELLY, R
*On the construct validation of comprehension tests: an exercise in
applied linguistics.* (PhD) University of Queensland, 1978.

MURPHY, D F and CANDLIN, C N
Engineering Lecture Discourse and Listening Comprehension. Practical
Papers in English Language Education, Vol. 2, pp. 1-79. (1979).

OLLER, J W, Jr and HINOFOTIS, F B
*Two mutually exclusive hypotheses about second language ability:
indivisible or partially divisible competence.* In: OLLER, J W, Jr
and PERKINS, K. Research in language testing. Rowley, Mass.:
Newbury House, 1980.

ISSUE OR NON-ISSUE:
GENERAL LANGUAGE PROFICIENCY REVISITED
Helmut J Vollmer, University of Osnabrück

At the time when I wrote my paper 'Why are we interested in 'General Language Proficiency'?' to be presented at an International Language Testing Symposium in Germany, I intended to clarify some of the basic claims and questions associated with that concept. I knew that Bernard Spolsky was going to take part in that symposium having been invited as the main guest speaker. I considered Spolsky to be one of the major proponents of that concept and was all the more surprised to find out that he was not any more, but was rather critical of the testing business altogether (cf Spolsky 1981).

In the meantime much discussion has been going on internationally and, equally important, substantial research results have been presented ever since. In addition, the methodological aspects of the issue have been elaborated upon and new theoretical advances have been proposed with the effect that no firm answer seems to be possible to the question 'Is there really only one single factor of language ability?' in the near future. I would not go as far as to assert that the issue of General Language Proficiency (GLP) 'is essentially a non-issue theoretically' (Davies,this volume), but it certainly has changed its quality and forcefulness as a research question: the discussion has led away from the macro-level of mathematical data reduction procedures to a psychologically more informed and better motivated information-processing view of language performance and to the intensive analysis of tasks and individual differences on a micro-level of behaviour.

In order to illustrate somewhat further what I mean by these general remarks I have divided my response into three sections:

1 Empirical findings
2 Methodological and theoretical advances
3 Final remarks.

Empirical findings

Much progress has been made during the past two or three years in proving that the structure of foreign language ability is not likely to be one-dimensional. As far as I can see no one seriously claims the Unitary Competence Hypothesis (UCH) to hold true empirically any more. On the contrary, even John Oller at a Testing Symposium held last summer (1980) at the University of New Mexico in Albuquerque, publicly admitted that he might have gone too far in postulating only one unitary, indivisible underlying ability all the different language activities a learner can engage in. It will be interesting to find out how far Oller has come to a substantial revision of his position in a new book edited by him on **Issues in Language Testing Research** to which the present author also has contributed (cf Vollmer/Sang forthcoming).

In my own research (done jointly with F Sang at the Max-Planck-Institut für Bildungsforschung in Berlin) I tried to demonstrate that the empirical evidence presented in a great number of studies does not really enable one to decide in favour of one or the other theoretical positions. On the basis of an extensive analysis and re-analysis of all the relevant factor analytic studies up to 1979 (including Gardner/Lambert 1965, Lofgren 1969, Caroll 1975, Oller 1976, Steltmann 1978, Sang/Vollmer 1978, Hosley/Meredith 1979, Oller/Hinofotis 1980, Scholz et al. 1980 among others) it was shown in particular that the strong versions of both hypotheses (unitary versus divisible competence) can hardly be justified and would clearly have to be rejected on the basis of the data available. It should be remembered here that according to the multidimensional model of foreign language ability several independent factors were expected, one for each single cell in the component-by-skill-matrix. The strong version of the UCH on the other hand asserted that only one GLP factor should appear, explaining the whole amount of common variance among all sorts of language performances. There seems to be no substantial support for either one of these two extremes (cf Vollmer 1980; Vollmer/Sang forthcoming).

It cannot be denied, however, that in a number of studies — either in its original form or even after the reanalysis — only one single strong factor remained (cf. Oller 1976, Sang/Vollmer 1978, Steltmann 1978, or as it were, Carroll 1975) explaining anything between 76% and 55% of the common variance. In all of these cases the appearance of a strong first factor could not be easily interpreted in terms of the UCH but was rather to be labelled as a 'pseudo-general factor' for several reasons. The number and range of variables investigated was lacking in all of the studies mentioned. In other words, important aspects of language behaviour (above all: the productive side of handling a language) were not included for consideration at all (or not sufficiently, at least). Moreover, the relatively small number of variables, highly correlated with each other, also meant that there was hardly any chance in factor analysis to divide those variables up in more or less homogeneous groups indicating dimensions of language proficiency. The probability for a one-factor-solution was rather high from the very beginning, without proving very much about the structure of the variables under investigation as it is (or might be) in reality. We would only consider it to be a clear piece of evidence for the assumption of one-dimensionability, therefore, when a one-factor-solution showed up even if a large number and a broad variety of tests were included in the analysis. Yet in a case like this the probability of the appearance of more than one factor will rise again: whenever twelve or even more language variables were included (Carroll 1958, Pimsleur et al. 1962, Gardner/ Lambert 1965, Lofgren 1969, Bonheim/ Kreifelts et al. 1979, Scholz et al. 1980) statistical analysis led to at least three different factors; but again, none of these structures found can be interpreted materially in terms of the strong form of the divisible competence hypothesis.

In order to arrive at a sound judgement on the dimensionality of language ability, one would have to include a variety of tests to measure productive performances, namely to assess writing and speaking skills on a somewhat discoursal and communicative level. As a guideline, one should perhaps measure the four integrated skills by at least three different methods/instruments each (combining various approaches and formats). In addition, we will have to take the necessary precautions to ensure that our samples are more or less homogeneous as to the range of previous experience and exposure, because heterogeneity of a population might very well lead to the appearance of an artificially strong first factor (without having a substantial meaning in terms of a structural hypothesis). In this connection it is also very important to make comparative studies between second language acquisition in a natural versus formal setting. It might be especially interesting here and worthwhile to find out how far the distinction between 'creative competence' and 'reproductive competence' (Felix 1977) seems to hold empirically.

As to our own (deficient) data (cf. Sang/Vollmer 1978, 1980) I (nevertheless) undertook a follow-up study trying to test alternative explanations for the appearance of such unexpectedly high inter-correlations between our six variables (Pronunciation, Spelling, Vocabulary, Grammar, Reading and Listening Comprehension). The rationale behind this procedure was finding out whether or not the correlations could have been 'produced' at least in part or even substantially by the influence of a third, intervening variable like motivation of the learner. Four groups of variables were investigated in relation to the proficiency measures:

> school setting, curriculum, teaching methods
> (complex versus simple skill approach)
> aspects of learner motivation (including achievement motivation and attitude towards school, preference of subjects and interest in learning the foreign language)
> intelligence
> achievement in the first language (German as mother tongue).

The results of this study cannot be reported here in any detail: the main findings, however, may be mentioned (cf. Vollmer 1980):

a The first three groups of variables hardly show any effect on the correlations between the language tests: neither is the amount of common variance explained by the first factor reduced in any significant way nor is the factorial structure itself affected at all.

b As soon as the influence of the first language (measured by an array of 11 different tests including knowledge of words and grammatical forms as well as discourse analysis) on the performance in the second language was controlled statistically, the average correlation between any two subtests in L2 went down from .45 to .28. At some time two factors emerged instead of one: the first one being interpretable as a dimension of complex skills in understanding (38.8%), the other one being associated with simple and basic knowledge in L2 and especially with 'Pronunciation' (16.9%). These results basically indicate that the linguistic and cognitive ability or abilities already built up in acquiring German as L1 heavily influence (but do *not* determine!) the learning of L2, namely the proficiency profile in English as a foreign language. Once the influence of L1 is controlled for, we are left with two factors to be interpreted as specific competencies having genuinely to do with L2. And these competencies seem to be more or less independent of one another (on the basis of a varimax rotated factor solution). A General Language Proficiency across L1 and L2 does not seem to exist.

Neither the quality of the tests used nor the data itself allow any stronger argument to develop at the moment. To be more explicit: The test results of L1 and of L2 have yet to be factor-analysed together. In addition, the two factors gained should not be mistaken as psychologically real abilities, but should be taken as a convenience, as handy constructs so far. What I simply wanted to demonstrate is the direction in which future research might advance. In this regard, I strongly agree with what was said in the Symposium discussion.

In view of all the empirical data we have so far, I have come to the conclusion that in all probability there is no such thing as a 'Unitary Competence' across languages. It also does not make sense to postulate the existence of two separate factors in the human mind, one GLP factor in the first language and one in the second. At least for the second language the UCH can hardly be upheld in the light of all the counter-evidence mentioned earlier.

Consequently, it might be worthwhile to consider other versions of unidimensional and multidimensional models which are less strong, which would have the advantage of being more plausible (at least from the data side) and thus being more acceptable (even as competing hypotheses).

The development of weaker forms of theoretical assumptions (as introduced by Cummins (1979), for example, in the case of Oller's UCH) seems promising and helpful in the attempt to give our research efforts a more productive focus.

It will also be necessary in the future to test another alternative: hierarchical models of foreign language abilities. These models might possibly offer a better explanation for the different sets of data given and might describe the structure of foreign language competence more adequately.

Methodological and theoretical advances

It might very well be that one of the greatest shortcomings in the analysis of linguistic and communicative competence is to be seen in the inappropriateness of the procedures applied in finding out about its structure. Too much concentration on factor analytic models is a case in point here. Only recently Upshur and Homburg (forthcoming) have demonstrated quite convincingly that the UCH is but one possible causal model among others and that this one-factor model is not at all the best fit to the data they investigated. In particular, they show how the choice of method is determined by the underlying theoretical model which is assumed to hold true.

In our own work (cf. Sang/Vollmer 1980; Vollmer/Sang forthcoming) we have been able to prove that the principal component data reduction procedures 'produce' quite different structural results than would be the case in aiming at principal factor solutions. This difference in method can lead to strikingly divergent interpretations of one and the same set of data as exemplified by the reanalysis of Oller/Hinofotis (1980) or Scholz et al. (1980): in each particular case it meant interpreting the data alternatively either **for** or **against** the UCH, depending on the analytical producedure chosen and the number of factors generated thereby. I therefore cannot agree with Davies, who considers this choice to be merely a matter of 'arithmetic elegance'. It definitely is not — at least not in the way it is sometimes handled in the literature.

But again this argument must not be exploited too far. Both types of factor analysis are generally used in a purely exploratory way and thus are good only for helping to generate hypotheses, but not for testing them. Accordingly, there have been two main objections as to the use of factor analysis: first, it produces a structure under almost any circumstances; secondly, it does not offer any criteria for determining whether the structure found is only a chance product or indeed a replicable representation of the domain under investigation. It is not at all clear, therefore, what the factors thus produced really mean, with no theory backing up any kind of interpretation. The only chance of reducing the risk that any factorial structure found is (mis)interpreted too quickly as a reflection of reality is to describe a structural hypothesis as detailed as possible **before** the analysis is begun. This chance, of course, is further narrowed down when only one factor is expected. But, independent of this expectation, the chosen type of method tends to maximise the variance among different language performances on the first factor anyway (this being true for the principal component as well as for the principal factor analysis). This is why the possibility of method-induced artefactual results cannot be ruled out in the case of a single-factor solution just as much as in the case of multiple-factor solution within classical factor analysis. In other words, the assumption of some sort of GLP factor being the simplest model under conditions given has always a fairly good chance of being verified — even if the model may not be an adequate representation of the relationship between the variables involved. These objections, however, do not hold good any more in the light of newer forms of the so-called 'confirmatory' factor analysis (used by Palmer/Bachman) which allow a statistical comparison between the predicted model and the results actually achieved. The same is true for path analysis as it is advocated by Upshur/Homburg (forthcoming).

Possibly we have been too much preoccupied with the assumption of factorial casuality, with the interpretation of factors as underlying abilities or 'latent traits' within an individual. This interpretation has been seriously questioned. Consequently, a critical reassessment of classical test theory as well as psychometric theory is under way. We are having to ask ourselves what our tests really measure.

In order to understand better this change of focus (or change of paradigm, as it were), it might help to look beyond the narrow borderlines of the language testing business. As early as 1977, R J Sternberg presented his componential approach to human intelligence. Sternberg elaborates on the severe intrinsic limitations and even misuses of factor analysis being the main tool within a differential approach to the human mind. He reminds us of an important distinction between two types of theory, the psychological theory and the mathematical one. 'The psychological theory states how the mind functions. The mathematical theory states the way a set of empirical data should look' (Sternberg 1977: 29f.). As to the limitations of factor analysis they are summarised as follows:

'First, the machinery of factor analysis rather than the investigator formulates and thus has control over the mathematical theory, resulting in a

200

reduced ability of the investigator to perform theory-comparison operations. Second, solutions are indeterminate because of the infinite number of possible axis rotations. Third, factor analysis is done over items, and hence cannot be used as a means for discovering or explicating the processes that are used in solving individual items. Fourth, intelligence and abilities exist within the individual, but factor analysis is between individuals (except in rare cases)'

(Sternberg 1977:36).

Sternberg continues by analysing the information-processing approach in its advantages and limitations on the other hand. He finds that it suffers from none of the intrinsic limitations of the factor-analytic method. Yet none of the three methodologies (computer simulation, subtraction method, additive-factor method) within the information-processing approach seems to '(1) provide a means for studying systematically correlates of individual differences in performance; (2) provide a common language across tasks and investigators; or (3) prevent overvaluation of task-specific components' (Sternberg 1977: 63).

The author therefore wants to synthesise an approach 'that would capitalise upon the strength of each approach, and thereby share the weaknesses of neither' (1977: 65). In his componential analysis of human intelligence the fundamental unit is the **component**.

'A component is an elementary information process that operates upon internal representations of objects or symbols . . . The component may translate a sensory input into a conceptual representation, transform one conceptual representation into another, or translate a conceptual representation into a motor output. Componential Analysis is therefore akin to information-processing analysis in that its elementary unit is a process rather than a construct representing a static source of individual differences' (Sternberg 1977: 65).

Factors then cannot be interpreted as 'latent traits', but rather as mathematical representations of 'reference abilities' defined as 'constellations of components that in combination form stable patterns of individual differences across tasks' (Sternberg 1977: 78). In this theoretical and methodological context a **general** component would be one which is 'mandatory in all tasks of a specified kind', whereas a **group** component is optional. 'It is used in only a subset (or group) of the tasks being considered' (1977: 319).

The implications of this componential approach for the study of foreign language proficiency/ability have only just begun to be investigated. In this situation we can only hope to progress somewhat further by combined theoretical efforts: What does it mean to know a language and to act in it from an information-processing point of view? What are the cognitive processes in understanding and producing meaningful utterances? For only when we develop a clearer picture of the individual strategies, processes, operations etc. as well as of the task-specific demands that are involved in foreign language learning and testing shall we be able to devise valid foreign language tests in the future.

Personally, I have been working on a componential model of foreign language ability during recent weeks. In comparing comprehension with production processes I am trying to show that their structural-procedural equality does not seem to be justified. Although the results of psycholinguistic research to date indeed suggest that the encoding and the decoding system in the human mind have much in common, production and comprehension as macro-activities can probably not be seen as mirror images. Attempts have been made to account for their unique characteristics by postulating specific as well as general underlying processes. As to the former, the role of inferencing as opposed to planning procedures is a case in point here. Generally speaking, the differences between knowing how to analyse input and knowing how to construct output apparently outweigh the correspondences between these two acts of discourse (for more details cf. my paper presented at the Lund AILA Congress, Vollmer 1981).

Final remarks

In my opinion, the concept of GLP, as defined by Oller, for example, has largely served its purpose. It has stimulated controversial debate and a lot of research activities and thereby provoked international communication of some width. Yet within the narrower boundaries of the problem as it was originally posed many an argument and some hard data have been put forward against the assumption of only one internal general factor of language proficiency. I cannot finish, therefore, without contradicting Davies in what he labelled the 'philosophical question' behind the GLP controversy: to him this question (general versus specific or unitary versus divisible competence) does not seem 'amenable to proof'; to me it **does**: the UCH can more or less be rejected on theoretical as well as empirical grounds (though more evidence is needed to strengthen the proof).

At the same time, the rejection of the UCH does not necessarily mean support for the multidimensional model of language ability in its strong form and traditional definition. As I tried to indicate above, the whole problem of (foreign) language proficiency (and of GLP, consequently) will have to be redefined in theoretical and methodological terms. This is not to say, of course,

202

that we do not need our philosophical strength and intuitive virtues any more. On the contrary, these should be applied to more promising issues on a less abstract level of investigation, eg what goes on in the learner solving a specific task, interacting with others in varying socio-linguistic contexts, trying to understand a specified topic, item, or text, reacting to it, organising his/her own thoughts and expressing these more or less adequately etc. It could very well be that in all these activities a number of processes are at work that are 'general' and 'differential' at the same time in the sense that in combination they form more or less stable patterns of individual differences across tasks and over time. Other processes may be more task-specific. A single component may enter into many different constellations of tasks and individual solutions thereof.

This **Componential view of language proficiency** needs to be elaborated upon before we can better judge its value. Certainly it is not the only view possible. A totally different approach to defining and measuring foreign language proficiency, namely **functional testing** (with its highly contextualised items, areas, and levels of performance and its notion of specific competencies for specific purposes) should likewise be followed through — for practical reasons just as much as for theoretical considerations. Both lines of development seem to be equally necessary.

BIBLIOGRAPHY

CUMMINS, J
Cognitive/academic language proficiency, linguistic interdependence, the optimum age question and some other matters. Working Papers on Bilingualism 19, 1979, 197 – 205.

OLLER, J W (ed)
Issues in language testing research. Rowley, Mass.: Newbury House (forthcoming).

OLLER, J W and HINOFOTIS, F B
Two mutually exclusive hypotheses about second language ability: factor analytic studies of a variety of language tests. In: Oller, J W and Perkins, K (eds.): Research in language testing. Rowley, Mass.: Newbury House 1980, 13 – 23.

SANG, F and VOLLMER, H J
Allgemeine Sprachfahigkeit und Fremdsprachenerwerb. Zur Struktur von Leistungsdimensionen und linguistischer Kompetenz des Fremdsprachenlerners. Berlin: Max-Planck-Institut fur Bildungsforschung 1978.

SANG, F and VOLLMER, H J
Modelle linguistischer Kompetenz und ihre empirische Fundierung. In: Grotjahn, R and Hopkins, E (eds.): Empirical research on language teaching and language acquisition. Bochum: Brockmeyer 1980, 1 – 84 (Quantitative Linguistics vol. 6).

SCHOLZ, G. et al.
Is language ability divisible or unitary? A factor analysis of twenty-two English proficiency tests. In: Oller, J W and Perkins, K (eds.): Research in language testing. Rowley, Mass.: Newbury House 1980, 24 – 33.

SPOLSKY, B
Some ethical questions about language testing. In: Klein-Braley, C and Stevenson, D K (eds.): Practice and problems in language testing I. Proceedings of the First International Language Testing Symposium, held at the Bundessprachenamt, Hurth July 29 – 31, 1979. Frankfurt, Bern: Peter Lang Verlag 1981, 5–21.

STERNBERG, R J
Intelligence, information processing, and analogical reasoning. Hillsdale, N J: Erlbaum 1977.

UPSHUR, J A and HOMBURG T J
Some relations among language tests at successive ability levels. In:
Oller, J W (ed.): Issues in language testing research. Rowley, Mass.:
Newbury House (forthcoming).

VOLLMER, H J
*Spracherwerb und Sprachbeherrschung: Untersuchungen zur Struktur von
Fremdsprachenfahigkeit.* Osnabruck 1980. (To appear in Tubingen:
Gunter Narr Verlag 1981).

VOLLMER, H J
*Receptive versus productive competence? — Models, findings, and psycho-
linguistic considerations in L2 testing.* In: Proceedings I: Sections and
Workshops of the 6th AILA Congress. Lund, Sweden 1981.

VOLLMER, H J and SANG, F
Competing hypotheses about second language ability: a plea for caution.
In: Oller, J W (ed.): Issues in language testing research. Rowley, Mass.:
Newbury House (forthcoming).

EPILOGUE
Arthur Hughes, University of Reading

The symposium, the structure of which is mirrored by this volume, dealt in turn with three closely related topics. As a result, the same or very similar issues tended to recur, not always in quite the same form, often without their interconnectedness being made explicit. The purpose of the epilogue is to provide a brief summary of these issues, to show how they relate to each other, and to suggest what part they may play in the future development of language testing. In order to do this, instead of treating separately each of the three topics, I shall base what I have to say on the criteria against which all tests, however novel or exciting, must be judged. These are, of course, validity, reliability, and practicality.

As Carroll himself says, the superiority of ELTS over the current test needs to be demonstrated. The ultimate criterion for a test like ELTS is that of **predictive validity**. Its superiority — if indeed it is superior — must be shown in terms of its ability to predict whether an applicant will be able to cope with the linguistic demands made on him by a particular course of study. The problems associated with such validation were discussed at the symposium. But whatever the difficulties, and however persuasive the arguments for giving the test the structure it has, its predictive power has to be demonstrated empirically. It would be particularly interesting to know if, for example, in predicting academic outcomes for science students, an ELTS with a second phase relating to science subjects would prove more accurate than one with a second phase relating to the social sciences. If it did, this would provide powerful support for ESP testing. Until the results of ELTS validation tests are known, however, we must suspend judgement. The ELTS test has a secondary, diagnostic function: to determine the nature and duration of the course of language instruction needed to achieve the required competence in the language. This function, too, is a predictive one and susceptible to similar empirical validation.

By contrast, the RSA test, with which Morrow is associated, to the best of my knowledge makes no claims to prediction. That test and other similar, 'communicative' tests must therefore be subjected to **concurrent validation**. Since there appear to be no comparable tests already validated, this must be based on something like the comparison of scores made on the test by a subset of candidates with ratings of their performance in an extended series of communicative tasks. Once more it has to be said that it is not rhetoric but only empirical validation studies which will convince us of the efficacy of new tests or testing methods.

The proposals that Carroll and Morrow make, and the arguments that they offer in their support, are concerned essentially with **content validity.** Morrow wants communicative language tests to sample the skills involved in communication, while Carroll intends the second part of the ELTS test to sample the tasks that will be required of students on various academic courses, with particular attention being paid to relevant varieties of English. As the symposium discussion revealed, representative sampling of these skills may be very difficult to achieve. For one thing, we lack thoroughly researched and sufficiently detailed analyses of students' language needs on whose inventories sampling might be based.[1] For another, despite Carroll's faith in Munby, we do not have a descriptive framework of language use comparable in completeness or systematicity to those we have of language form; nor do we have anything like a full understanding of the relationships holding between even those elements and dimensions of language use with which we are reasonably familiar. If, however, Carroll and Morrow are successful in their sampling — if, that is, they can predict from the sample of responses obtained in the test to the population of responses in which they are interested — then not only will their tests have greater predictive or concurrent validity (other things being equal), they should also have a beneficial effect on language teaching.

The lack of a demonstrably valid conceptual system on which to base tests of language use, referred to above, may be remedied, at least in part, by **construct validation** studies. If we follow Cronbach (1960) rather than Davies (1968), construct validation is seen as the empirical validation of an interpretation (expressed in terms of underlying concepts) of performance on a test. As such, it may not have immediate appeal to those who regard themselves as 'practical testers' rather than 'testing theoreticians'. Nevertheless, the results of construct validation studies may have important implications for test construction. The better we understand just what underlies performance on language tests, the more confidently we can build new, appropriate tests for particular purposes. The recent upsurge of interest in construct validation owes much to Oller and his promulgation of the Unitary Competence Hypothesis. Verification of this hypothesis would seem to undermine the positions taken in their papers by Carroll and Morrow. In fact, even though research carried out by Oller and his associates has tended to support the hypothesis, there has been criticism (some of it in this volume)

---

[1] Weir is at present working on a large scale study of the language needs of overseas students on behalf of the Associated Examining Board. It remains to be seen what part his analysis will play in the construction of a proposed new examination for such students.

of the methodology and materials used in these studies, as well as of the interpretation of their results. Palmer and Bachman's paper presents counterevidence; and since the symposium Hughes and Woods (1981) have found as many as four statistically significant components underlying performance on the Cambridge Proficiency Examination. In stimulating so much research, however, Oller has made an invaluable contribution to language testing. It is to be hoped that the current enthusiasm for construct validation studies continues. A great many candidates for investigation, such as **enabling skills** and **language varieties,** have presented themselves in this volume.

A word ought to be said about **face validity.** While face validity is sometimes dismissed as not 'real' validity, it is of undoubted importance in test design. A test's lack of face validity will have a detrimental effect on predictive or concurrent validity; at least some candidates will fail to take the test seriously, and so their performance on the test will not provide an accurate picture of their ability.

There ought to be no argument about the need for test **reliability.** Measurement cannot be consistently accurate if it is not reliable. It may be easier to achieve reliability through the use of a great many discrete items and of techniques which permit objective scoring. But we know that through careful sampling, marking scales based on well defined and recognisable levels of ability, and multiple assessment, it is possible to obtain high reliability for essay questions and interviews. It seems unlikely that problems arising from the techniques to be used in the new communicative tests will not be amenable to similar solutions. The reliability coefficients of these tests will tell us how successful their constructors have been in finding them.

The final criterion is that of **practicality.** Tests cost money to construct, administer, score and interpret. ESP testing implies more tests — and so greater costs — than general proficiency testing; and the achievement of reliability in the assessment of language production skills will be more expensive than is the case with multiple-choice tests. At the same time it has to be recognised that valid tests may save money. If the ELTS test proves successful, one administration might easily save several thousand pounds (and avoid the waste of a year or more of the applicant's life!). We must realise that the weighing of such savings against costs incurred may be as influential in the development and use of new tests as the skills and knowledge of test constructors.

Throughout the symposium, as in this epilogue, there were repeated calls for more research. In their excitement the participants even promised to do some of it themselves. It is only through continued research (in the broadest sense) that the current level of interest in language testing will be maintained or even increased. It is in recognition of this that a BAAL (British Association for Applied Linguistics) seminar on language testing research, with sections parallel to those of the symposium, is to be held at Reading University in December, 1981. And it is to promote the rapid dissemination of ideas and information on tests and testing research, and to encourage co-operation between researchers, that a Language Testing Newsletter has been established.[2]

As Alderson says in his introduction to this volume, a very great many people have a contribution to make to the future development of language testing. It is hoped that the reader will recognise himself as one of their number.

BIBLIOGRAPHY

CRONBACH, L J
Essentials of Psychological Testing (second edition) New York, Harper and Brothers, 1960.

DAVIES, A, *ed*
Language Testing Symposium. Oxford University Press, 1968.

HUGHES, A and WOODS, A J
Unitary Competence and Cambridge Proficiency Paper presented at AILA Congress, Lund, August, 1981.

---

[2] Information on the Newsletter can be ĥad from the writer, at the Department of Linguistic Science, University of Reading, Reading, RG6 2AA.